BEHOL. DULCE

Record of ET–Trafficking

from History-to-Now

by

THE INVESTIGATORS :: Bennett, Bennowitz, Branton, Burisch, Cooper, Costello, Dobbs, Hall, Hamilton, Janitch, Lear, Lee, Leir, Lieder, Meier, Moret, Moulton-Howe, Steiger, White et al.

ILLUSTRATED

ANTHOLOGY chronology, edited &

set to QUESTIONS by

Emily Windsor-Cragg, BS MA

Yuba-Sutter County CA 95991

May 7, 2018

ACKNOWLEDGMENTS

Some people care what is true and what is not true,
care more about that than they care about what OUGHT to
be true.

This compilation of first- and second person Sources comes
out of the Bill Cooper generation of experiencers.

These are the people who put their lives on the line to say
what was going on before their eyes.

Those are the people we thank in our prayers, who have
paid the final price for knowing.

NON-ACKNOWLEDGMENTS

The holes in the fabric of information are larger than the
patches of knowledge, no thanks to the mainstream media,
no thanks to Hollywood, no thanks to Silicon Valley, no
thanks to the Vatican, no thanks to Masonic Orders, no
thanks to Church communities, no thanks to Institutes, nor
to Charities, nor to Academic Institutions, nor to Federal
Departments.

PREFACE

"BEHOLD! A PALE HORSE," is being revived. What Cooper tells us is that our National Governance structure has split apart over the issue of Non-Human Races and the Interventions of the same in our world and our society. But Mainstream Media, Academic and Hollyweird only display and articulate subjective and speculative questions—never real facts, the real deal we adult Humans must confront.

This volume is the Addendum to Cooper's "BEHOLD! A Pale Horse," quotations authored by a dozen or so of his contemporaries., in the manuscripts Dulce, Charles Hall's Tall Whites' Story, in Dan Burisch's accounts, of Robert Leir, John Lear and so many others who put their lives on the line in order to tell the Truth.

There are several compelling reasons why these materials have to come out ~NOW~. 1) Because most of this information is 40-20 years old, and we have no access to more recent data. 2) Because social media—GOOGLE, FACEBOOK & YOUTUBE--are methodically deleting and censoring these material facts from their archives and 3) we have a Presidential Administration facing a reality in which he is draining a swamp, but we don't know whether or how much he knows about this situation.

My Apologies.--These accounts are more-or-less organized in chronological order, quotes-within-quotes, overlapping; so I removed most of the quotation marks. I use the word, "A-liens" everywhere and "Greys," just to be consistent. I quote whole paragraphs, intact, leaving authors and subjects in place. I hope the resulting sequence of events and problems makes sense.--*Editor*

UFO / ET INTERVENTIONS videos

https://youtu.be/4TQNaml_WcM -- 2014 Govt Psychothronic Weapons

https://youtu.be/nCT5D6U8GYw -- 2014 ... People Vanishing

http://youtu.be/o1dWcryO6Co -- 2013, Part 1 . . .Alien Attack

https://youtu.be/2tZZkVLpUGA Part 2

https://youtu.be/-lj2afg31oU – 2011, When Aliens Attack

https://youtu.be/-lAK_XLZMX0 -- 2011 Experiments Exposed, Cloning etc., Jim Corbett

https://youtu.be/o1dWcryO6Co -- 2011 .Speculation of a "Human Alien War" in a D.U.M.B. near Los Alamos N.M.

LINK http://youtu.be/8mPZlvsCAm0 -- 2011. Obama Justifies FEMA imprisonment of civilians!

https://youtu.be/LLCF7vPanrY -- 2010 Time Lapse Map of Every Nuclear Explosion

https://youtu.be/ux_Zkqc79gA -- 2010 Scientific Study of Alien Implants

https://youtu.be/-lj2afg31oU -- 2011 When A-liens Attack (full video)

https://youtu.be/xl8S6SOPPWM -- 2011 a True Tale of Repeated Alien Contact

https://youtu.be/8Xm5zgvwMo8 -- 2009 Underground cities aren't for dummies

LINK http://youtu.be/FZ-LGbatyio – 2009 Obama depopulation exposed

https://youtu.be/uEDAE_9v4h0 --2008 D.U.M.B.s Deep Underground Military Bases

http://www.infobomber.org/2008/11/08/eugenics-the-secret-agenda/ . . . Eugenics the Secret Agenda, text

http://www.a-w-i-p.com/index.php/2010/07/08/the-case-for-war-the-iron-mountain-report – 1976 A Case for War, Iron Mountain Report text

LINK http://youtu.be/uRP8C2xpyEQ – 1765 The U.S. Constitution was plagerized from Native Americans

*Links originate from www.Abidemiracles.com, most are gone.

THE SECRETS OF THE MOJAVE :

DULCE & ET-TRAFFICKING

Conspiracy Against Reality

Compiled by 'A Group' headed by "Branton"-- *Bennett,*
Bennowitz, Burisch, Cooper, Costello, Dobbs, Hall, Hamilton,

1

Janitch, Lear, Lee, Leir, Meier, Moulton-Howe,Steiger, White et al.

"And I will show wonders in the heaven above... and signs in the earth beneath... blood, and fire, and vapour of smoke..." -- Acts 2:19 –

SECTION 1 – 500,000 years ago to 6000 years ago

According to Billy Meier, Pleiadeans come from the Tau Ceti and Epsilon Eridanus star systems, which are two of the nearest SOL-type star systems in this sector of the galaxy. A great interplanetary battle and mass human exodus took place ages ago from the Lyran system, and as a result a large percent of the human inhabitants were forced to evacuate Lyra within that system after Most of them perished in The Thousand Years War against Draconis.

2

Billy Meier was not told, to our knowledge, just who the 'attackers' were, but another 'contactee' claims that the attackers in the 'Lyran wars' were none other than the interstellar parasites known to us as the Greys. Humans who have been abducted against their will by the Greys have even been shown holographic recordings of such an interplanetary war, as if Greys in their leviathan pride were parading their supposed invincibility to their frightened and confused abductees.

One interesting thing that Meier was told is that Nordics and Pleiadeans are approximately 3000 YEARS advanced over us in technological development. Extreme closeness in development between the three constellations of Taurus (Pleiades), Cetus, and Eridanus (adjacent to each other and in the same sector of the sky) when compared to the multi-billion year history of the Universe is reflected in that nearly all human cultures in this sector of the universe who have contacted eartheans claim to be no more than a few thousand years advanced over us.

The most likely explanation is that human life in this part of the galaxy appeared on one single world and quickly spread out to other systems, adapting themselves to their new environments, especially after "hyperspace" travel became a reality.

As a result of the Lyran Wars, according to Meier, a leader by the name of Pleiore allegedly led a mass exodus of surviving refugees from the Lyran system in an effort to reach and colonize the Pleiades, the Hyades and Vega. Even today as we've seen previously, some Contactees reportedly encounter modern-day Vegans as well as Pleiadeans. At this

3

point in time, Meier was told, the Pleiadeans were part of a union of interstellar colonists and civilizations numbering over 127 billion humans.

Are there any other accounts that might support the above scenario?

Yes, Voyagers II by Anna Yates.

One can only assume that if certain humans would 'sell out' their own kind to an alien race and use such an infernal alliance to gain dominion over their fellow man, then they should consider the fact that they, according to universal law, must in the same way open themselves up to being manipulated and controlled by their supposed benefactors.

As it is written, "the servant is not greater than his lord." There are indications that an ante-diluvian race *(the Annunaki*—Editor) or races attempted this very same thing a couple of hundred thousand years ago, after the flight from Lyra.

Construction of vast subterraneous [*and subsea*] systems like the ones now being built by the more modern secret societies clearly commenced when mankind still had access to stone technologies, magnetics and astronomy from ET Progenitorsw.

There are also indications that later societies and their underground networks intersect these ancient antediluvian excavations and outposts: e.g., Sumerian, Egyptian Inca, South African. This is evidenced by the many accounts which describe how Masonic-related secret societies utilize both the ancient and modern sub-systems related to ET conquest.

4

Many indicators, stories and accounts also point to the continuing speculation that entire human colonies, both peaceful and alien controlled, may covertly exist within deep levels of the Earth's crust. These colonies are allegedly inhabited in part by ancient native American or meso-American tribes or explorers who crossed the seas from ancient Mediterranea and elsewhere in the eastern hemisphere thousands of years ago.

These may also include more recent (past few centuries) American inhabitants or explorers of Anglo-Saxon descent as well. Indications are that such explorers happened to discover some of these ancient antediluvian excavations, which led to deep tunnel networks and ancient hydrothermal and geothermal cavities containing conditions sufficient to sustain physical life.

Ancient North American History

The author of the following story is a Navaho Indian. He revealed this tribal secret which he learned from the Paiute Indians, who inhabit the Great Basin and Mojave deserts of Utah, Nevada, and California.

This native American, who went by the name Oga-Make, related the following account in appreciation for a story on the Navaho which appeared in the Spring of 1948 in a magazine which was carrying numerous articles on the mysterious signs or fires in the skies which were causing an enormous amount of confusion and debate during that same year, as well as the years following.

The article in the *Navaho Nation* told of the suffering that their tribe had gone through during past winter seasons, and encouraged the readership to send goods and supplies to help them through the upcoming winter of '48-'49, which many of them did.

In appreciation for this generosity, Oga-Make their Chief related the following 'legend' which told of the secret history of the Americas which ran its course, possibly thousands of years before white men set their foot en masse upon its shores:

Most of you who read this are probably white men of a blood only a century or two out of Europe. You speak in your papers of the Flying Saucers or Mystery Ships as something new, and strangely typical of the twentieth century. How could you but think otherwise?

Yet if you had red skin, and were of a blood which had been born and bred of the land for untold thousands of years, you would know this is not true. You would know that your ancestors living in these mountains and upon these prairies for numberless generations had seen these ships before, and had passed down the story in the legends which are the unwritten history of your people. You do not believe? Well, after all, why should you? But knowing your scornful unbelief, the storytellers of my people have closed their lips in bitterness against the outward flow of this knowledge.

Yet, I have said to the storytellers this: now that the ships are being seen again, *is it wise that we, the elder race, keep our knowledge to ourselves?* Thus for me, an American Indian, some of the sages among my people have talked; and if you care to, I shall permit you to sit down with us and listen.

Let us say that it is dusk in that strange place which you, the white-man, calls 'Death Valley.' I have passed tobacco . . . to the aged chief of the Paiutes who sits across a tiny fire from me and sprinkles corn meal upon the flames ...

'We, the Paiute Nation, have known of these ships for untold generations. We also believe that we know something of the people who fly them. They are called The Hav-musuvs.'

'Who are the Hav-musuvs?'

'They are a people of the Panamints, and they are as ancient as Tomesha itself.' "He smiled a little at my confusion.

You do not understand? Of course not. You are not a Paiute. Then listen closely and I will lead you back along the trail of the dim past.

When the world was young, and this valley which is now dry, parched desert, was a lush, hidden harbor of a blue water- sea which stretched from half way up those mountains to the Gulf of California, it is said that the Hav-musuvs came here in huge rowing-ships. They found great caverns in the Panamints, and in them they built one of their cities. At that time California was the island which the Indians of that state told the Spanish it was, and which they marked so on their maps.

Living in their hidden city, the Hav-musuvs ruled the sea with their fast rowing-ships, trading with far-away peoples and bringing strange goods to the great quays said still to exist in the caverns. Then as untold centuries rolled past, the climate began to change.

The water in the lake went down until there was no longer a way to the sea. First the way was broken only by the southern mountains, over the tops of which goods could be carried. But as time went by, the water continued to shrink, until the day came when only a dry crust was all that remained of the great blue lake. Then the desert came, and the Fire-God began to walk across Tomesha, The Flaming-Land.

'When the Hav-musuvs could no longer use their great rowing-ships, they began to think of other means to reach the world beyond. I suppose that is how it happened. We know that they began to use flying canoes. At first they were not large, these silvery ships with wings. They moved with a slight whirring sound, and a dipping movement, like an eagle.

'The passing centuries brought other changes. Tribe after tribe swept across the land, fighting to possess it for awhile and passing like the storm of sand. In their mountain city still in the caverns, the Hav-musuvs dwelt in peace, far removed from the conflict. Sometimes they were seen in the distance, in their flying ships or riding on the snowy-white animals which took them from ledge to ledge up the cliffs. We have never seen these strange animals at any other place. To these people the passing centuries brought only larger and larger ships, moving always more silently.'

'Have you ever seen a Hav-musuv?'

'No, but we have many stories of them. There are reasons why one does not become too curious.'

'Reasons?'

'Yes. These strange people have weapons. One is a small tube which stuns one with a prickly feeling like a rain of cactus needles. One cannot move for hours, and during this time the mysterious ones vanish up the cliffs. The other

8

weapon is deadly. It is a long, silvery tube. When this is pointed at you, death follows immediately.'

'But tell me about these people. *What do they look like and how do they support themselves?*'

'They are a beautiful people. Their skin is a golden tint, and a head band holds back their long dark hair. They dress always in a white fine-spun garment which wraps around them and is draped upon one shoulder. Pale sandals are worn upon their feet...'

The preceding account, titled "Tribal Memories of the Flying Saucers", appeared in the Sept. 1949 issue of *FATE Magazine*. Coincidentally or not, this same 'legend' was repeated in amazing similarity by an old prospector by the name of Bourke Lee in his book *Death Valley Men* (Macmillan Co., New York, 1932).

The story of the Hav-musuvs seems to be a major or key piece of the overall puzzle of a wide range of aerial as well as subsurface phenomena which have mystified numerous researchers throughout this century.

Not the least of these unusual phenomena were the so-called contactees of California who during the 1950's and '60's, in fact, described their own alleged encounters with 'benevolent' human-like beings who were seen to emerge from aerial disks, not far at all from the mysterious Pana-mint mountains them- selves.

The Mojave Desert is also, believe it or not, the very place where William Shatner claimed to have had his UFO encounter with a silvery disk, which he alleges saved his life after he became lost in the Mojave's other-worldly expanse,

9

and this long before he was Christened 'Captain' of the U.S.S. Enterprise!

The Mojave Desert of California is perhaps one of the most interesting areas in the world whereas encounters with strange aerial phenomena are concerned. In certain small California and Mojave Desert towns, like the small town of Anza for instance, one is more likely to be called crazy for NOT believing in UFO's than they are for believing in them. Sightings have been so numerous over the years that these aerial visitors are an accepted fact of life.

The interesting thing, however, is that the two most commonly reported types of occupants who are described by thousands of witnesses with remarkable consistency the world over (in relation to these aerial phenomena) play a large part in the Mojave Desert scenario as well. These are the two groups which have often been referred to at the Saurian Greys and the Nordic Blondes.

Both types of entities appear in many accounts of encounters with not only extra-terrestrial beings, but also the lesser known--although nevertheless persistent-- accounts of intra-terran beings as well. In this file we will document numerous accounts which seem to suggest that Nordics [redheads in North American Great Lakes region] may be our ancient ancestors who, a few thousand years previous to the modern space race, may have attained the science and technology necessary to burrow deep into the earth in order to construct vast subterranean tech- nological metropolises, and shortly thereafter like a slingshot from the lower depths of the earth they may have hurled themselves

10

in starships of their own devising through the interplanetary and perhaps even interstellar depths of space.

Ancient sophisticated artifacts discovered imbedded in SOLID ROCK (including ancient spark plugs, metal cubes, gold chains, metal vases, nails, screws, and even electric batteries such as those described in Rene Noorbergen's, *Secrets of the Lost Races*, Bobbs-Merril Co., N.Y.), as well as artifacts found on the ocean floor, give evidence to the fact that our ancient ancestors were FAR more intelligent in the scientific realm than we give them credit for. Yves Naud, in his book, *UFO's and Extra-terrestrials in History* (Ferni Publishers Geneva, Switzerland, 1978)

Many American subterranean networks, before the turn of the century (1900), were apparently inhabited mostly by human societies; yet it seems as if a Reptoid invasion of the sub-strata of North America occurred en masse in the early part of the 1900's, with a major push into the U.S. subnet from already-occupied underground systems in Central and South America taking place around 1933.

This movement according to many accounts involved Reptoid beings who had been in possession of underlying cavern networks beneath Asia and the Far East; and according to their imperialistic-predatory nature these creatures began expanding their influence into the Western Hemisphere—first into Central and South America and finally North America itself. Some unconfirmed reports tell of whole groups of humans (both surface exploration parties or even troglodytical tribes) who were wiped-out in sudden attacks by the serpent race in a type of battle beneath the earth.

Centuries ago, surface people (some say Illuminati) entered into a pact with an Alien nation hidden within the Earth. The U.S. Government in 1933 agreed to trade animals in exchange for high-tech knowledge and to allow "Them" to use (undisturbed) some underground bases in Western U.S.A. A special group was formed to deal with Alien beings.

It is said that, in the 1940's 'Alien Life Forms' (ALF's) began shifting their focus of operations from Europe, Central and South America to the U.S.A. The continental divide is vital to these entities, because magnetic substrata rock and high energy plasma states have been known and utilized from long ago. The North American southwest has a very high concentration of lightning activity as well, which ET's need and can use; underground waterways and cavern systems facilitate their occupancy; fields of atmospheric ions serve as source of energy.

The following excerpt is taken from an article by TAL LeVesque entitled, 'The Covert Return of an Alien Species of Reptoid Heritage—the Dulce Base," that appeared in a mailer-newsletter sent by researcher Patrick O'Connel to TAL--

Ages ago a competition with other beings (ELs) destroyed most of their [Reptoid] civilization and forced some of them into deep caverns & others to leave earth entirely, fleeing to Alpha Draconis and/or Altair in the constellation Aquila (which in ancient lore was home of predatory Reptoids). . . . The conflict was a Species War-of-Predation **upon** the Edamic Seed **by** the Serpent (Draconian) Seed.

(Note: Researcher Maurice Doreal claims this predation took place by giant humans or 'ELs' working with pre-Nordics based in the Gobi region of Asia several thousand years ago, and it included Reptoid hominoids based in Antarctica! - *Branton*)

Aside from human and Reptoid entities, there are some who speak of a third type of being, a hybrid between Humans and Reptoids. Some feel a cross between the two could never be produced; however, fossil evidence shows that "variforms" have existed from Eternity til now; and we know from history that the Annunaki are themselves a mixed Race, although Galactic Dogma [the El-Anu Treaty] provides that ONLY White Races shall ever "ascend," leaving hybrids in a Soul situation of No Future Life except as Clones [as the Greys must do].

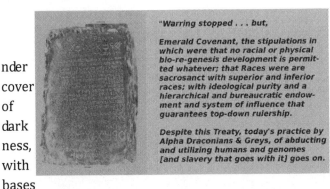

"Warring stopped . . . but,

Emerald Covenant, the stipulations in which were that no racial or physical bio-re-genesis development is permitted whatever; that Races were are sacrosanct with superior and inferior races; with ideological purity and a hierarchical and bureaucratic endowment and system of influence that guarantees top-down rulership.

Despite this Treaty, today's practice by Alpha Draconians & Greys, of abducting and utilizing humans and genomes [and slavery that goes with it] goes on.

nder cover of dark ness, with bases hidden inside the earth, nocturnal invaders have chosen to reclaim what was once theirs & use it (and us) as a staging area in their ancient conflict with the 'ELs'. That is to say, Reptoids wish to reclaim what they wish us to believe was once theirs. (The 'ELs' are the so-named EL-der race, a human-like culture tied into the Edamic heritage yet who

13

have retained a very tall physical stature, in some cases being twice as tall as the average International or surface Terran. Due to their physical differences, they have chosen to inhabit exterran and subterrane; belonging to other dimensional realms so as not to induce irrational fear or worship of themselves by their more diminutive human cousins, whom we are. – Branton)

Do benevolent human-A-liens allegedly working at the Nevada Test Site have any connection with Hav-musuvs describe7d earlier? Were human-occupied bases on Luna (as seen by NASA officials and according to George H. Leonard and others), actually installations placed there by the Havmusuvs or another society affiliated with them long long ago?? Hmm. Consider

Reptoids or Lizard-like beings similar to those described above have been seen in deep underground tunnel networks below the general southwestern areas of Albuquerque (especially Dulce and San Crystobel), New Mexico; Las Vegas (especially Groom Lake), Nevada; Salt Lake City, Utah; and within caves in the Black Mountains between Las Vegas, Nevada and Kingman, Arizona.

The joint interaction program between Draconis and Agarthians or Adamic White stock began because they need to develop aspects of advanced technology, so certain humans in key positions of power within government, military, corporations, 'secret societies', are contacted telepathically, and led along. . . . Human population as a whole began to be manipulated into the Alien Agenda when ordinary people began to question official policy dogma,

14

question effects and outcomes. . . . when the Man on the Street see "They" want total control over us, you and me.

The reason hybrid Races are desperate to engineer DNA is so it can serve as an Eternal Life platform for them, which most of them do not have because they are not part of eternal Covenants expressed as Ascension and Salvation. You see, under the Emerald Covenant, El-Anu Treaty, genetic engineering is forbidden; however, it is pursued in earnest by those Races and ideologies that violate El Anu sanctions against Racial mixing, and mixed Races and they have no chance at an Eternal incarnate manifestion, none at all.

F. W. Holiday, in his book, **The Dragon and the Disk** (W.W. Norton & Co., Inc. New York, N.Y. 1973) relates the unusual facts concerning relationship between serpent or 'dragon' legends and the modern 'UFO' phenomena wherein Satanism and Luciferianism--that is to say, the religion of the dragon—takes hold in times of decadence and judgment. These individuated belief systems were contemporaneous between the Annunaki Princes Enki and Enlil and in Babylon and Bronze Age Britain. In both branches of thought culling is practiced by minority groups cut off from Cosmic relationship in order to curry favor with powerful demons; so officialdom and political correctness embrace dragon religions only in times of disorder and chaos.

When Cryus occupied Ur . . . a form of dragon-worship seems to have been in vogue there. The priests of this cult escaped the Persians by fleeing north with their Pontiff (or *Pontifex Maximus*, a position which has allegedly been secretly held in an unbroken chain from Babylon up to modern times - *Branton*) into the mountains of Asia Minor. The followers of Satanism finally came to rest at a place called Pergamos in Lydia (western Turkey) and there set up a religious centre which became known as 'Satan's seat'. St. John said: 'And to the angel of the church of Pergamos, write: These things saith He [God] which hath the sharp sword with two edges [judgment and mercy]: I know they works, and where thou dwellest, EVEN where Satan's seat is...'

The Romans also knew about Satan's seed and annexed it into their empire after the death of Attalus III, the last of the Pergamite kings. About this period a plague broke out in Rome and prayers were offered to the Roman gods in vain. It was decided, therefore, to appeal to Satan at Pergamos. The symbol of the cult is always a serpent and a special ship was sent to Lydia to transport the god to Rome. (Most likely it was a depiction or idol representation of the god, in that idols among early pagans were indistinguishable from the so-called gods themselves - *Branton*) There it was installed as a deity with great pomp and circumstance.

The disease had probably run its course and the resulting improvement in public health was attributed to Satan. The new religion was so popular that snakes of inoffensive species were allowed to glide around at parties -- at least so Seneca says. In Historia Augusta they are called *Dracunculi* or little dragons.

The Aesculapian Serpent -- as the 'god' was called -- is shown on a carving at Pompeii and is unlike anything known to herpetologists. It had vertical humps and snail-like horns, exactly like the monsters (sea serpents - *Branton*) of Scotland and Ireland. A bronze Urarian cauldron in Rome carries the erect head and neck of the creature modeled in the round. It is hideous. It has a shovel-like mouth, bulging eyes and tentacles or sensory-organs hanging on each side of the face.

No-one, of course, thought that snakes were dragons. The malignant Great Serpent of Babylonia was TYPHON or Teitan, Satan, the author of wickedness. . . .Politicians, however, never look a gift-horse in the mouth as long as it produces results. After giving the Roman people carnage in the guise of circus entertainment, there was no reason for the emperors to shrink from a little devil-worship.

Even the national flag was given the treatment. Ammianus Marcellinus describes the standard 'purpureum signum *Draconis*'. And when Julius Caesar appeared in full regalia as the *Pontifex Maximus*, he was dressed in reddish-purple robes the same as the Pergamite dragon-priests. The reader can trace the rest of the story in Gibbon's 'Rise and Fall of the Roman Empire.'

In his book, **The Serpent and the Satellite**, (Philosophical Library, New York), author F. Alfred Morin reveals on page 343:. . In Jewish legends the serpent is sometimes described as a modified Reptoid human-like creature indicating that this description was also gradually evolving into the symbolism of wickedness or Satan into the image and likeness of a man.

Dragon-worship persisted long after Christianity and Catholicism were proclaimed and established. Tertullian complained: 'These heretics magnify the serpent to such a degree as to prefer him even to Christ himself; for he, they say, gave us the first knowledge of good and evil.' There is a case to be argued that demons, dragon monsters and U.F.O.s are in some way linked, correlated or connected by chains of causation, we're not sure.

Mojave mysteries are NOT known only to small groups of researchers who meet in secret to discuss their latest findings. The subject of aerial and subsurface populations is gaining more prominence as more evidence and documentation comes to light. Major motion picture studios are interested in the phenomena, in order to cash in on Government secrecy and forbidden histories.

John A. Keel, American journalist who delves into these mysteries, talks about a conspiracy. He warned me: 'Proceed with caution in your Loch Ness work. We are caught up in a series of games which must be played by the rules. Anyone without Cosmic protection who tries to invent his own rules or breaks the basic pattern soon loses his mind or even his life'.

When Jesus sojourned in this world, for instance, he condemned the serpent as being in league with fallen angel Satan [who taught Self-Service and promised followers they would have supernatural power and authority over these serpents if only they would put their trust in His Word. - *Branton*). Lucifer came later, who teaches ideology-first-Ethics. Those who believe this is dramatic and silly may care to remember the words of St. John: "And he doeth great wonders, so that he maketh fire to come down from heaven on the earth in the sight of men and deceiveth them that dwell on the earth by The means of those miracles which he had power to do in the sight of the Beast."

The beast that performed miracles was what the Jews called 'The Shining One', 'The Great Serpent' and 'Satan'. If this is the underlying truth of the phenomena, then Keel's warning is by no means too strong.

In relation to the above, during Dark Ages of Roman Rule, early Dracologists documented many accounts of battles between knights and dragons or winged and limbed serpents. An infestation as it was called by the early chroniclers, conflict was allegedly halted with the advent of the spread of Christianity, and the worms as they were often referred to were forced to retreat back into the underworld from which they had emerged by valiant Christian Knights such as St. George and Lancelot, who vanquished beastly enemies at every turn.

The Mojave Desert of Southern California and the deserts of western Nevada may in fact be a secret and continuing battleground involving U.S. Government troops working allied with the Race known as Nordics (particularly on the issue of genetic engineering and transhumanism) struggling against Saurian Greys and Satanic [Globalist] infidels. This war, according to several sources is against Greys' cross-breeding experiments and cloning efforts— seen as unholy and outlaw--that have over the last century (possibly earlier) drenched the underground bases in the Mojave Desert region and elsewhere, in blood and misery.

UFO Sightings Reported

In 1905 an 'airship flap' was observed throughout southern California. On August 2, 1905, J. A. Jackson,a well-known resident of Silshee, was out at 1:30 in the morning when a bright light appeared in the sky and headed for him. According to an account published in the Brawley, California, NEWS on Aug. 4, 1905:

He watched it closely until behind the light there appeared the form of an airship, apparently about 70 feet in length, with a searchlight in front and several other lights aboard. The mysterious machine appeared to be propelled by wings alone and rose and fell as the wings flapped like a gigantic bird. Apparently there was no balloon attachment as is usually the case with airships.

Mr. Jackson, being close to the home of W.E. Wilsie, aroused and woke up his friend in time to see the lights of the machine before it disappeared... The same night, H. E. Allatt, postmaster at Imperial, was awakened from sleep by a bright light shining into his room. There was no moon, the light was thought to be fire, and Mr. Allatt rose to investigate, but no fire was found. Looking at his watch, the time was discovered to be 1:30 a.m., and it is believed that the brilliant light was caused by the searchlight from this mysterious airship.

A craft of almost identical description was reported only four years later in the Dec. 15, 1909 issue of the Arkansas GAZETTE:

A. W. Norris of Mabelvale, road overseer of District No. 8, is of the opinion that an airship passed over his residence at about 10 o'clock Monday night (December 12). Mr. Norris states that he was standing in his doorway when a strange light appeared, apparently about 300 feet above him, traveling south at a rapid rate of speed and disappeared a moment or two later in the darkness. He said that the light had the appearance of a searchlight similar to those used on automobiles, and IT ROSE AND FELL like a bird in flight. The night was cloudy, which precludes the possibility of the light having been a star or any atmospheric phenomena.

Air ships of this description were apparently common following the turn of the century, but few if any of this particular type of craft have been reported after the period just described (1900-1910, etc.).

Just because an 'airship' appears over California or Arkansas does not necessarily indicate that the airship was native to either one of those areas. However, there are nonetheless many reports, as indicated elsewhere in this File, that the Mojave Desert--Panamint Mountains -- Death Valley areas were apparently (in ancient times) a 'cradle', possibly one of many, for an early civilization which later developed an advanced form of technology; and having done so in relative secrecy, they were unhindered by the 'uncivilized' tribes outside of their domain who continued in their relatively ignorant lifestyles.

Just as the U.S. government has been working with 'Nordics' based at Mt. Shasta near Weed, California and others in nearby star systems such as those mentioned above who have a base below the Panamint Mt.-Death Valley region; the neo-Saurian colonies are allegedly working with others of their kind within a huge subterranean network centered below the Mt. Archuleta region near the town of Dulce in Northwestern New Mexico (which seems to be the U.S. Center of activity in regards to MIBs or 'Men In Black', abductions, mutilations, disappearances, sightings of Reptoid entities and so on).

Greys and other Draconians have established themselves in Alpha Draconis, Epsilon Bootes, Zeta Reticuli, Altair

21

in Aquila, Rigel and Belletrax Orion, as well as possibly other nearby star systems. *Why is such aa 'war' being carried on in secret today?* Partly because the U.S. Government does not believe the American public can handle the truth about this. Just recall Orson Wells' *'War of the Worlds* radio program of so many years ago, and the panic it incited.

William Cooper continues, writing about the 1954 Treaty negotiations with President Eisenhower:

"...The A-liens showed a hologram, which they claim was the actual crucifixion of Christ. The Government filmed the hologram. We did not know whether to believe them.

A symposium was held in 1957 which was attended by some of the great scientific minds then living. They reached the conclusion that by, or shortly after, the year 2000 the planet would self-destruct due to increased population and man's exploitation of the environment without any help from God or A-liens.

By secret Executive order of President Eisenhower, the Jason Scholars were ordered to study this scenario and make recommendations from their findings. The JASON Society confirmed the findings of the scientists and made three recommendations called for Alternatives 1, 2, and 3.

Alternative 1 was to use nuclear devices to blast holes in the stratosphere from which the heat and pollution could escape into space. They would then change the human cultures from that of exploitation into cultures of environmental protection. Of the three this was decided to be the least likely to succeed due to the inherent nature of man and the additional damage the nuclear explosions would themselves create.

Alternative 2 was to build a vast network of underground cities and tunnels in which a select representation of all cultures and occupations would survive and carry on the human race. the rest of humanity would be left to fend for themselves on the surface of the planet. We know that these facilities have been built and are ready and waiting for the chosen few to be notified.

Alternative 3 was to exploit the alien and conventional technology in order for a select few to leave the earth and establish colonies in outer space.

And in reference to her 'Negro Project' of the late 1930's, which aimed at recruiting black ministers, physicians and political leaders for the purpose of encouraging birth control and sterilization in the black community, the Feminist Sanger wrote: "...We do not want word to go out that we want to exterminate the negro population, and the minister is the man who can straighten out that idea if it ever occurs to any of their more rebellious members." - *Branton*). Cooper continues:

"The joint U.S. and Soviet leadership dismissed Alternative 1 but ordered work to begin on alternatives 2 and 3 virtually at the same time. "

Conflict Local or Conflict Galactic?

Perhaps the most remarkable confirmation of this situation appears in Bourke Lee's biography, **Death Valley Men** [MacMillan Co., New York. 1932], which also dealt with caverns within the Panamint Mts. region. If indeed the Panamint mountains are an ancient 'doorway' to advanced and hidden Human civilizations, then one must recognize that it--as well as any of it's national treasures--should be (as

23

should be any national border) considered legal territory of those who have possessed it since ancient times.

But are Borders entirely horizontal, or are they vertical as well?. Unwelcome intrusions into such undiscovered territory underground can be dealt with as in any other nation on earth or in space;, and one ought to approach the question, *"Which land is whose?"* with caution. Unlike other areas where subterraneous and harmful or dangerous (Reptile) behavior is likely to occur, we must consider the natural inter-dependence and national sovereignty of those subsurface regions also. Hidden Human colonies may reside also underfoot; and these should be honored as one would honor ANY national border on the face of the earth.

Even if an archeological discovery surfaces which belonged to ancestors of ancient culture that still exists, that discovery should be the property of that culture alone. One of the arguments for making the public sensitive to information on various exterran and subterran cultures would be for the protection of Humans who venture in. Secret government machinations, by bringing international public condemnation against any Race or hidden culture and its right to maintain their dominion, liberty and autonomy . . . is a matter for Law to determine and resolve. If Law fails, then War is the outcome.

If the secret government knowingly violates another country's rights, every other independent country in the world may feel threatened as well. And in the case of the various hidden underground centers utilized by Reptoid Greys, public knowledge of this fact is necessary to maintain national security of each independent culture which might otherwise be infiltrated by implantation or by signal, which inevitably leads to other forms of intrusive control--political, spiritual, educational, economical, etc.).

Even IF various subsurface human cultures were driven out of their underground homes and if those cultures can somehow regain their homeland by counter-invasion against Reptoid incursions, then those territories will come under legal question, not merely be the objects of war and conflict. Ownership must be deserved, to manifest Good.

Supposing there is a counter-invasion in the future, there is still be much territory left over, so one Culture driven out implies they must mobilize and leave, or fight on. A cave-dwelling tribe, colony or culture in underground systems might then be claimed by an outside government if they felt the need to expand their own territory.

According to some accounts, the U.S. government does know about many such underground systems and having found many of them unoccupied in past explorations, have claimed them for their own. What this comes down to is one conclusion. The matter of Ownership of Land is not adequately provided for, in Law, given the existence of land wars as these.

Underground repositories of ancient artifacts and ancient treasures have been melted down by prospectors, tomb robbers, etc., in order to gain the metal value of the gold, silver and other precious metals, out of which the ancient artifacts were formed, in order to prevent the State from pirating the find away from its finders. By doing so, the immense historical and archaeological value of such treasures is destroyed in exchange for the relatively pitiful metallic value. Many of the ancient Egyptian treasures fell prey to such vandals and 'grave robbers' in ancient times. Even if one does not agree with the religious symbolism behind such artifacts, their historical and archeo- logical value makes them nevertheless worthy of preservation.

The only reason that King Tut's treasures have made such an impact (even though he was a minor 'king'), is that these treasures were among the very few which were not discovered by grave robbers and melted down for their metal content.

There is no telling how much historical information about ancient cultures has been forever lost by such careless actions. Hopefully humankind has reached the point of maturity where the discovery of such treasures in the future will result in a cooperative scientific study of the ancient artifacts for the benefit of all, rather than the violence, death and betrayal which has often resulted in the past through the mistakes of selfish treasure hunters fighting each other for the 'booty'. According to some accounts many of these ancient sites still await discovery, and finds which may make King Tut's Tomb look insignificant by comparison may still await discovery.

As we have implied, just as one should honor the ancient archaeological sites of existing cultures, in the same way one should honor the national sovereignty of another human culture itself. To fail to do so would be in essence to discard any legal argument a nation might have for the protection of their own national sovereignty

(CASE IN POINT: the Reptoid or Draconian Empire with its major earth-center in the Bhoga-vita complex below

India, as well as the human Illuminati empires on and beyond earth--that apparently have a secret alliance with each other—have so interfered in the sovereignty of nearly every nation on earth, they have done so to the point that they can no longer legally claim any rational defense against any nation which that would confront them.

The Reptoid empire is of course a problem in itself, having been at war via overt attacks or covert manipulation against the majority of humanity in, on, and above earth since ancient times. And apparently, from the accounts given throughout this and other files, Draco-Grey-Bavarian partisans do not even acknowledge humankind's right to this world, nor even our 'right' to exist in light of "population reduction" tactics they have wrought and placed over Humanity..

Paihute Indian legends say that the 'People of the Panamints' long ago left their ancient city within the mountains of California and moved most of their civilization into still deeper cavern levels, and according to still other accounts—moved to colonies beyond the confines of planet earth itself. Although those Havmusuvs may have been more benevolent in comparison to othrs, they nevertheless, according to documentation in this and other databases, have the ability and technology to defend their borders and their loved ones from potential enemies.

In his chapter 'Old Gold' the author of '**Death Valley Men**', Bourke Lee, relates the allegedly-true account of two prospectors who claimed to have discovered this ancient, abandoned city within huge caverns inside the heart of the Panamint mountains. Take special note of the incredible similarity between this account and the one given to the Navajo Oga-Make by an old Paihute sage, as recorded in the article 'Tribal Memories of the Flying Saucers'. We will take up the story where two Death Valley residents by the name of Bill and Jack are having a conversation with two prospectors, 'Thomason' and 'White', from whom the author apparently learned the details of this place is in Death Valley.

In the late 1920's, right in the Panamint Mountains, found by accident, a Mr. Thomason was prospecting down on the lower edge of the range near Wingate Pass. He was working in the bottom of an old abandoned shaft when the bottom fell out and landed him in a tunnel.

We've explored the tunnel since. It's a natural tunnel like a big cave. It's over 20 miles long. It leads all through a great underground city; through the treasure vaults, the royal palace and the council chambers; and it connects to a series of beautiful galleries with stone arches in the east slope of the Panamint Mountains.

Those arches are like great big windows in the side of the mountain and they look down on Death Valley. They're high above the valley now, but we believe that those entrances in the mountain side were used by the ancient people that built the city.

Humans today deal with propaganda and intimidation rather than listen to stories of old men. Or today, we play video games. But one source believes ALL Saurian-Greys or EBE's come from extraterrestrial worlds. Others think the evidence shows that Saurian activity exists within deep sub-terranean levels and cavities throughout the earth, and has so for many centuries. It's hard to say, or know.

28

Saurians (and Bigfoot) hide from humankind, both terrestrial and extraterrestrial. Also, there are accounts suggesting that Sauroids, Greys, etc., are in fact breeding profusely and reproducing themselves via deep subterranean polyembryony tanks below Dulce and elsewhere, and are not as 'over-extended' as they might have us to believe. You can take it either way.

However, on the other hand, a fear the humans might have prematurely attacked enemy positions might possibly be propaganda intended to keep humans from taking offensive action, believing they are keeping the Greys, etc., 'at bay' when in fact the Greys are attacking human society offensively on other hidden fronts via mass abductions, deception, implantations, psychic manipulation, recruitment of fifth column humans and infiltration. Again, it's hard to know what's true.

A man by the name of Morris Doreal, also of Colorado (a state which is or was believed to be the home of an advanced subterranean human culture), runs an organization called the 'Brotherhood of the White Temple'. Doreal claims to have visited a few of the ancient underground cities and alleges that several members of his organization are Guatemalan Indians of Mayan descent who have told him of their own knowledge of subterranean cities inhabited by both good and evil beings—hominids or humans or whatever.

It is true that there are many strange caverns in the regions of Yucatan and Guatemala. Eastern Guatemala has 'Silpino Cave' which has allegedly been explored extensively in the direction of ancient volcanic cones without any daring

Spelunkers ever finding an end to the labyrinth. Even so, the Loltun Caves of Yucatan have an even more interesting history, being surrounded with accounts of ancient treasure troves, endless passages, encounters with people within its depths who claim to be centuries old, and even stories of lost tribes who vanished into the depths while fleeing their enemies, never to be seen again. Now back to the subject of the Hav-musuvs and the mysterious Mojave and Death Valley region.

One might ask: *If some of our ancient ancestors were so intelligent that they could develop aerial craft, then where is all the evidence?* The evidence is there, but has been largely ignored by orthodox scientists who cannot fit the existence of advanced prehistoric civilizations into their own theoretical framework.

To be sure, hiding underground is an expression of a Suspicious outlook toward one's fellow man. And, under-standably it has apparently led many subterranean cultures to develop technologies in secret. Some hidden societies such as the MIB or Men In Black are defensive of intrusion and have used a type of psychological terrorism in order to keep their secrets hidden from those on the surface, especially now that the technologies of 'International' societies are refined.

Now back to the subject of the Illuminati conspiracy and its alleged connection with aerial and subsurface phenomena. There are some researchers who believe, aside from the revelations above, that there is a definite connection between the 'Illuminati' and the alien group known to many researchers as the 'Men In Black'.

Jim Brandon, in his book *Occult America* tells of an alleged underground installation below Washington D.C. known as 'NOD'. The present inhibitors of this subterranean installation are allegedly an underground race of 'power-trippers' tied into the highest levels of the NSA-CIA, who are in turn in contact with Sirius Star People or a group that some UFOlogists believe is the extraterrestrial extension of the Illuminati, also known as the 'Men In Black' or the 'Nation of the Third Eye'.

The 'NOD' and other similar facilities are reportedly NOT inhabited by ante-diluvians, but by people who later discovered these abandoned underground installations as well as the ancient technologies left there, which they learned to manipulate for good or evil. Brandon also mentions ancient tunnels discovered beneath Washington D.C. that have been investigated by government scientists, some of which, according to still other sources, contain walls with a glass-smooth but metal-hard glaze.

Such defensiveness and paranoia on the part of the MIB might be explained by their own guiltiness which stems from their ancient associations with the serpent races, and the subsequent mental control which Reptoids establish throughout their own and other 'collaborative' societies. Many MIB' however are prisoners of environmental influence and cannot be condemned for being born into such a society. There is no telling how many times such a scenario (of a society discovering the utilization of electro- magnetic energy and subsequently dis-connecting themselves from mainstream society) has run its course throughout the millennia.

As for Men In Black, which according to researchers like John Keel are an Illuminati-like secret society who may be collaborating with malolents Reptoids, their Black Automobiles have been seen entering and leaving underground areas, for example, one witness said--a particular mountain near a road that runs between Hopland and Lakeport California is a road on which many cars including government vehicles have allegedly disappeared throughout the years.

But whether good or evil, there are apparently numerous societies--many of them highly advanced technologically and many of them very ancient--who have hidden themselves away from mainstream surface societies, again for either benevolent or malevolent reasons. There is, in fact, evidence that such high-tech ancient cultures did exist in ancient times:

Ancient peoples knew about the atom, *but were they capable of producing an atomic explosion?* Scientists spent a long time wondering about this question until the discovery of the "Drona Parva," a Hindu text which recounts the explosion of an atomic bomb:

A flaring projectile with the brilliance of a flame without smoke, was launched. A great darkness suddenly obscured the skies. Clouds thundered in the uppermost air, releasing a downpour of blood. Burned by the heat of this arm, the world appeared shaken by fever"

Indeed, traces of artificial radioactivity have been detected in various parts of the world in the course of diggings into antique sites. In India a skeleton was exhumed which revealed a powerful intensity of radioactivity. This would tend to confirm the theory of atomic explosions in prehistory." Mr. Naud concludes.

Daniel Cohen, in his book, **The Ancient Visitors** (Doubleday & Co. Inc., New York. 1976), reports "A number of ancient epics from India contain descriptions of fiery flying chariots. There are lines like this one--'Bhima flew with his Vimana on an enormous ray which was brilliant as the sun and made a noise like the thunder of a storm.'"

Were the Chijnese on the Moon 4000 years ago? - Those ancient people, making use of their astronomical knowledge, report--

The way was long, and as if enveloped in darkness, explains Chu Yan, a Chinese poet of the third century B.C. Chinese tradition narrates the extraordinary adventure of Hou Yih, an engineer of the Emperor Yao, who decided, 4,300 years ago, to go to the moon with a 'celestial bird.' In the course of the flight, the bird indicated to the traveler the exact movements of the rising, the apogee, and the setting of the sun. Hou Yih thereafter explained that he 'sailed up the current of luminous air.' Could this current have been the exhaust of a rocket?

He saw an horizon which appeared frozen. To protect himself from the glacial air, he built the Palace of the Great Cold. His wife, Chang Ngo, left to join him on the satellite, which she described as a luminous sphere, brilliant as glass of an enormous size, and very cold.

Quoting from another Chinese legend:

33

The Mao-tse were (a) perverted race which had taken refuge in the caverns. It is said that their descendants still live in the outlying areas of Canton. Then, under the influence of Tchu-Yeo, they stirred up trouble throughout the world, and it became ridden with highwaymen. The lord Chan-Ty (a king of the so-called 'divine' dynasty) saw that the people had lost every vestige of virtue. And so he ordered Tchang and Lhy to cut all communication between heaven and earth. From that time on there was no more going up nor coming down.

SECTION 2 : THE 1940s

"The United States had developed, used, and was the only nation on earth in possession of the atomic bomb. This new weapon had the potential to destroy an enemy, and even the Earth itself. At that time the United States had the best economy, the most advanced technology, the highest standard of living, exerted the most influence, and fielded the largest and most powerful military forces in history.

Between January 1947 and December 1952 at least 16 crashed or downed alien craft, 65 bodies, and 1 live alien were recovered. An additional alien craft had exploded and nothing was recovered from that incident. Of these events, 13 occurred within the borders of the United States, not including the craft which disintegrated in the air. Of these 13, 1 was in Arizona, 11 were in New Mexico. Sightings of UFOs were so numerous that serious investigation and debunking of each report became impossible, utilizing the existing intelligence assets.

... Cover-up was initiated soon after the Roswell, N.M. crash. We wanted to know - 1) Who they were, 2) Why they were here, 3) How their technology worked. The cover-up became a matter of NATIONAL SECURITY (a blanket word covering secrecy and deception).

The live A-lien that had been found wandering in the desert from the 1949 Roswell crash was named EBE. The name had been suggested by Dr. Vannevar Bush and was short for Extraterrestrial Biological Entity.

EBE had a tendency to lie; and for over a year would give only the desired answer to questions asked. Those questions which would have resulted in an undesirable answer went unanswered. At one point during the second year of captivity he began to open up. The information derived from EBE was startling, to say the least. This compilation of his revelations became the foundation of what would later be called the 'Yellow Book.' Photographs were taken of EBE which, among others, I was to view years later in Project Grudge.

The cover-up involves secret organizations within our government such as MJ-12, PI-40, MAJI, Delta, the Jason Scholars, & known intelligence organizations such as Naval Intelligence, Air Force Office of Special Investigation, the Defence Investigative Service, the CIA, NSA, and more!

It involves think tanks such as RAND, the Ford Foundation, the Aspen Institute, & Brookings Institute. It involves corporations such as Bechtel, GE, ITT, Amoco, Northrup, Lockheed, & many others. It involves secret societies who may be the hidden bosses of the orchestrated events (i.e. economic collapse, wars, assassinations, conspiracies to manipulate & control humans & thereby to exercise enormous power over the destiny of the human race) - the Illuminati, Masons, Knights of Malta, etc.

Individual players are too numerous to list. The whole of this conspiracy forms an interlocking nexus. The goal is said to be a one world government (or Dictatorship)!

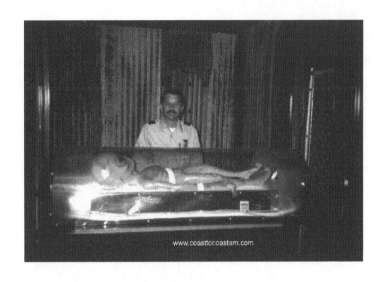

SECTION 3 : THE 1950s

In late 1951 EBE became ill. Medical personnel had been unable to determine the cause of EBE's illness and had no background from which to draw... Several experts were called in to study the illness. These specialists included medical doctors, botanists, and entomologists. A botanist, Dr. Guillermo Mendoza, was brought in to try and help him recover. Dr. Mendoza worked to save EBE until June 2, 1952, when EBE died. Dr. Mendoza became the expert on at least this type of alien biology. The movie E.T. is the thinly disguised story of EBE.

In July 1952, a panicked government watched helplessly as a squadron of 'flying saucers' flew over Washington, D.C., and buzzed the White House, the Capitol Building, and the Pentagon. It took all the imagination and intimidation the government could muster to force that incident out of the memory of the public."

L et's just take a look at som e actu al statements from those involved with these projects . . . From *THE UFO ENCYCLOPEDIA.*

"When four sit down to conspire, three are fools and the fourth is a government agent." -- *Duncan Lunan*

"The flying disks are real." -- *General Nathan Twining.*

According to Mr. ...informant, saucers were found in New Mexico due to the fact that the Government has a very high-powered radar setup in that area and it is believed that the radar [EM beams] interferes with the controlling mechanism of the saucers...

"Each one of the three saucers were occupied by three bodies of Human SHAPE, but only 3 feet tall, dressed in metallic cloth of a very fine texture." -- FBI Memo from agent Guy Hottel, Washington Field Office., sent to Director, FBI., March 22, 1950

"I would say that we know of several--should we say-- intergalactic fights that have taken place -- dogfights." -- United States Army Sgt. Clifford Stone, Roswell N.M. Station.

Because of developments of science all the countries on earth will have to unite to survive and to make a common front against attack by 'people' from other planets," Mayor Achille Lauro of Naples, quoting General Douglas MacArthur in the *NYTIMES*, Saturday Oct. 8, 1955. p. 7.

Thousands of sightings occurred during the Korean War and several more saucers were retrieved by the Air Force. Some were stored at Wright-Patterson Air Force Base, some were stored at Air Force bases near the locations of the crash site. An occasional saucers is so enormous and the logistic problems in transportation so enormous it must be buried at the crash site and remains there.

Stories are legendary on transporting crashed saucers over long distances, moving only at night, purchasing complete farms, slashing through forests, blocking major highways, sometimes driving 2 or 3 lo-boys in tandem with an extra-terrestrial load a hundred feet in diameter. (It is claimed, ALPHA or BLUE Teams out of Wright-Patterson AFB were the ones who were most often mobilized to carry out "crash-retrieval" operations. - *Branton*)

The newly elected-President in 1953 was General of the Army, Dwight David Eisenhower. "During his first year in office, 1953, at least 10 more crashed discs were recovered along with 26 dead and 4 live A-liens. Of the 10, 4 were found in Arizona, 2 in Texas, 1 in New Mexico, 1 in Louisiana, 1 in Montana, and 1 in South Africa. There were hundreds of sightings."

"The Underground Nation," The RAND symposium held on Deep Underground Construction allowed information that plans were hatched during the 50's to build underground bases, laboratories, & city-complexes linked by a stupendous network of tunnels to preserve and protect the ongoing secret interests of the secret societies. These secret societies made a pact with alien entities in order to further motives of domination." (*Bill Hamilton*)

Actually, as it turns out, They (secret societies) are now being dominated by the Other Worlders. Hamilton continues:

Underground complexes are not confined to the U.S. alone! A large underground complex operated by the U.S. exists at Pine Gap, near Alice Springs, Australia" (Note: According to various sources, conditions in this complex are somewhat similar to those at Dulce, that is, this underground base contains replicated flying 'disks' based on A-lien technology, and many workers there have allegedly been implanted and operate under a type of mental control of the Secret Government and Gray A-liens which also reportedly utilize the base as part of the Illuminati-Gray joint interaction – *Branton*).

As Bill Cooper relates the story in detail:

In the meantime, a race of humanoid (Nordic-Blond? - *Branton*) A-liens landed at Homestead Air Force Base in Florida and successfully communicated with the U.S. government.

A third landing at Muroc, now Edwards Air Force Base, took place in 1954. The base was closed for three days and no one was allowed to enter or leave during that time. The historical event had been planned in advance. Details of a treaty had been agreed upon. Eisenhower arranged to be in Palm Springs on vacation. On the appointed day the President was spirited to the base. The excuse was given to the press that he was visiting a dentist. Witnesses to the event have stated that three UFOs flew over the base and then landed. Antiaircraft batteries were undergoing live-fire training and the startled personnel actually fired at the crafts as they passed overhead... the shells missed and no one was injured. This 'meeting' apparently resulted in the Greada 'U.S. government – Gray & Annunaki' Treaty.

President Eisenhower met with the A-liens on February 20, 1954, and a formal Treaty between the alien nation and the United States of America was signed. We then received our first alien ambassador from outer space. He was the hostage that had been left at the first landing in the desert. His name was 'His Omnipotent Highness Crilll or Krilll,' pronounced Crill or Krill.

It was agreed that each nation would receive the ambassador of the other for as long as the treaty remained in force. It was further agreed that the [Grey-Annunaki] nations and the United States would exchange sixteen personnel with the purpose of learning about each others' cultures. The ET guests would remain on earth. The human guests would travel to their distant point of origin for a specified period of time, then return at which point a reverse exchange would be made. A reenactment of this

41

event was dramatized in the movie, *Close Encounters of the Third Kind.*'

It was agreed that bases would be constructed underground for the use of *alien nations* and that **two bases would be constructed for the joint use of the alien nation and the United States Government.** Exchange of technology would take place in the jointly occupied bases. *These joint bases would be constructed under Indian reservations in the Four Corners Area of Utah, Colorado, New Mexico and Arizona,* and one would be constructed in an area *known as Dreamland* (Note: Many sources allege that the reason the A-liens insisted on these underground bases beneath these particular areas was that those areas were already in use—for centuries—by underground Races that occupied deep cavern levels under the earth, and more recently beneath these areas of the southwestern U.S. [**Behold!**, *ibid.*]

The bases then, which most in the government might believe are of exclusively human construction for use in joint operations, would actually be 'covers' or 'fronts' for actual subterrain systems largely under the control of this Saurian race. *This would explain why--*

• many human workers in these 'joint' bases have been kept highly compartmentalized;

• why many do not realize what's taking place in the LOWER levels or even how many lower levels exist;

• why the 'security' increases enormously the deeper one descends into these underground bases;

42

• and why the human influence decreases and the Saurian-Reptoid-gray influence increases the deeper one descends into under-ground networks. (*Branton*).

Dreamland was built in the Mojave Desert near, or in, a place called Yucca. More ufo sightings and incidents occur in the mojave desert of california than any other place in the world--so many in fact—that no one even bothers to make reports. Anyone who ventures into the desert to talk to the residents will be astounded by the frequency of activity and with the degree of acceptance demon- strated by those who have come to regard UFOs as normal.

All A-lien areas are under complete control of the Naval Department (although some may argue that they are only in control of the uppermost levels of these bases-- *Branton*). Large donations of cash were made available in 1957. Work continued on the Yellow Book.

Project Redlight was formed and experiments in test-flying alien craft was begun in earnest. A super-Top Secret facility was built at Groom Lake in Nevada in the midst of the weapons test range. It was code-named Area 51. The installation was placed under the Department of the Navy and all personnel required a 'Q' clearance as well as Executive (Presidential, called *Majestic*) approval. This was ironic, due to the fact that the President of the United States does not have clearance to visit the site.

The alien base and exchange of technology actually took place in an area code-named Dreamland above ground, and the underground portion was dubbed '*the Dark Side of the Moon*.' At the time of installation at least 600 non-human ET personnel actually resided full-time at this one site, along with an unknown number of science professionals. Due to fears around implantation and mind controls only certain categories were allowed to confront and converse with the EBEs and their Grey Staffers, all of whom were monitored continuously

A multi-trillion-dollar Secret fund was organized and kept by the Military Office of the White House—namely—from the 50s on, by the drug trafficking network of the CIA. This fund and whatever moneys could be stolen from the Pentagon and the Atomic Energy Commission were used to build 75 underground facilities and the transport network between and among them.

Presidents who asked were told the fund was used to build deep underground shelters for the President in case of war. White House staffers in charge of the fund were aligned with George H W. Bush—from the Eisenhower Administration forward—and his Zapata Oil Company, by whom the drugs were shipped. When Bush became Director of the CIA, drug trafficking spread worldwide.

By 1955—**only one year later**--it became obvious that the A-liens had deceived Eisenhower and had broken the treaty. Mutilated humans were being found along with mutilated animals across the United States. It was suspected that A-liens were not submitting a complete list of human contacts and abductees to Majesty Twelve and it was suspected that not all abductees had been returned. The Soviet Union was suspected of interacting with them, an this proved to be true. The A-liens stated that they had been, and were then, manipulating masses of people through secret societies, witchcraft, magic, the occult, and religion. You

44

must understand that this claim could also be a manipulation. After several air force combat air engagements with alien craft it became apparent that our weapons were no match against them.

By secret Executive Memorandum NSC 5511 in 1954 and 1955 NSC-5412/2 in 1955 was issued establishing a study committee to explore 'all factors which are involved in the making and implementing of foreign policy in the nuclear age.' This was only a blanket of snow that covered the real subject of study, the alien question. The study groups were to 'examine all the facts, evidence, lies, and deception and discover the truth of the alien question.'

"Nuclear Weapons & Foreign Policy," published for the Council on Foreign Relations by Harper & Brothers, New York, was the supposedly the product of those meetings, delivered; however. In truth, the manuscript had already been 80% written while Kissinger was at Harvard. He had made up his mind what to do without reference to current condions or facts.

A major finding of the alien study was that the public could not be told. Another major finding was that the A-liens were using humans and animals for a source of glandular secretions, enzymes, hormonal secretions, blood plasma and possibly in genetic experiments.

The A-liens explained these actions as necessary to their survival. They stated that their genetic structure had deteriorated and that they were no longer able to reproduce. They stated that if they were unable to improve their genetic structure, their race would soon cease to exist.

45

We looked upon their explanations with suspicion (Note: According to sources , the actual purposes of the mutilations are far different from what these alien creatures allege them to be. Some groups connected to MJ-12 however seem to have fallen for this propaganda.)

For instance the top secret 'Yellow Fruit' unit working in Nevada has been, or at least were at one point, convinced that the Greys were incapable of reproducing themselves here on earth. In spite of 'their' allegations that the Greys or EBE's cannot reproduce, certain witnesses have alleged that the Saurian Greys are actually multiplying generously within deep underground levels where they utilize solar-heat 'egg' hatcheries, poly-embryony tanks, cloning, etc. Indeed, they are prolific.

Also body fluids, according to other sources, are not used exclusively for 'improving their genetic structure' but as sustenance or 'food' for the Saurian Greys, and possibly their 'Repton' superiors as well. (Their claims to the contrary, as well as other allegations, should be studied in the light of their previous known "*Tendencies to Lie*," ibid., *Branton*).

The ruling powers decided that one means of funding the alien-connected and other 'black' projects was to corner the illegal drug and guns markets. The English and the French had established a historical precedent when they exploited the opium trade in the far east and used it to fill their coffers and gain a solid foothold in China and Vietnam, respectively.

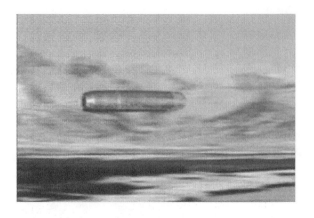

These are Alpha Draconis vehicles, at all times 'tubes.'

SECTION 4: THE 1960s

In the April, 1963 issue of SEARCH Magazine, Will Carson and Jeannie Joy, in their regular column '*Prying into the Unknown*', related the following incredible story, which involved an apparent encounter with an unknown race below the MOJAVE Desert region:

47

While exploring for petroglyphs in the Casa Diablo vicinity of Bishop, California, Mr. & Mrs. P.E. came upon a circular hole in the ground, about nine feet in diameter, which exuded a sulfurous steam and seemed recently to have been filled with hot water. A few feet from the surface the shaft took a tangent course which looked easily accessible and, upon an impulse with which we cannot sympathize, the dauntless E.'s, armed only with a flashlight, forthwith crawled down into that hole.

At a certain depth we failed to record the oblique tunnel opened into a horizontal corridor whose dripping walls, now encrusted with minerals, (and) could only have been carved by human hands, countless ages ago - of this the E.'s felt certain. The end of the short passage was blocked by what seemed to be a huge doorway of solid rock which, however, wouldn't yield. The light of their flash was turned to a corner where water dripped from a protuberance - which proved to be a delicately carved face, distorted now by the crystallized minerals, and from whose gaping mouth water issued.

As Mr. and Mrs. E. stood there in silent awe - wondering what lay behind that immovable door - the strangest thing of all happened...but our chronology will not be incorrect if we wait till they return to the surface before revealing this, for now the water began gushing from the carved mouth and from other unseen ducts elsewhere in that cave and rising at an alarming rate!

They hurried to the surface, and in less than half an hour there was only a quite ordinary appearing pool of warm mineral water on the desert floor.

48

'Do you know,' Mrs. E. asked to her husband, 'while I stood down there I heard music - the strangest, most weird music I'd ever heard. But it seemed to come from everywhere at once, or inside my own head. I guess it was just my imagination.'

Mr. E. turned pale. 'My God,' he said; 'I thought it was my imagination, but I heard it, too - like music from some other world!'

Why do they call that rock formation near where the E's had their strange experience Casa Diablo - the Devil's house? And why did the Indians name that area Inyo - dwelling place of the great spirit?

Nov. 1963.--From the time of the Kennedy Assassination, The Office of Majesty Twelve was a front; its coffers very limited, that financed lawful space contracts. It was used to build Top Secret alien bases as well as Top Secret DUMB (Deep Underground Military Bases) and Alternative 2 contracts. President Johnson used this fund to build a movie theater and pave the road on his ranch. He had no idea of it's true purpose.

In the early 60s subsurface researcher Richard Toronto reprinted a news article in his "Shavertron" News-letter describing a Municipal Water Director in Los Angeles. This official talked with a man who said that he was hired by the government to look for underground water sources for Camp Irwin in California.

At one point the man and a partner came across an abandoned mine and decided to follow it to the bottom. Near the bottom he was surprised to discover an ancient earth-fault which was wide enough for him and his companion to enter. They traversed this fault for a good distance until they finally emerged into a huge river-cavern. To his surprise he saw before him a crystal pure underground river over a quarter of a mile wide which flowed through the passage and out of sight.

Since learning of this incident the Municipal Water Director claims to have discovered at least five similar under-round rivers. Some of these have allegedly been die-traced and were found to emerge from the continental slope below the surface of the oceans, and at least one of them into the Gulf of California.

In 1962, a researcher by the name of Chuck Edwards released some of his own discoveries concerning what might be referred to as the 'Western Subsurface Drainage Network', which seems to cover parts of Utah, Nevada, and Southern California, where are located many drainage systems which do not ultimately flow into the Pacific ocean (via surface rivers, that is), but instead make their way underground into a vast subterranean drainage network.

His letter appeared in issue A-8 of '*The Hidden World*', one of the few specialized publications which grew out of the Palmer-Shaver controversy of 1940-45 which appeared in *Amazing Stories* science fiction/science fact magazine.

A controversy arose around Richard Shaver's claim to have inside knowledge of two subterranean Races which possessed aerial disks: the 'Deros' which have been vari-ously described as a race of ancient out-of-control Atlantean robots, degenerate human troglodytes, or a race of Reptoid non- humans (or all three) who were at war with another much more benevolent (and human) subterranean race discussed below.

This might confirm the claim made by one anonymous retired Navy officer that the Navy has knowledge of a VAST system or labyrinth of aqua-caverns which meander beneath the surface of California and even into other western states, and that these watery labyrinths exit out into the oceans via huge entrances in the lower walls of the Continental Slope.

Some mariners testify that is that some of these aqua-caverns are so large that they can be navigated by submarine, and that one nuclear submarine on a secret mapping mission in fact became lost within the maze and was never heard from again. Two American nuclear submarines have disappeared without explanation in the past, the *U.S.S. Scorpion* and the *U.S.S. Thresher.* The *Thresher* incidentally disappeared on April 10, 1963, with a crew of 129 men under the command of John W. Harvey, USN.

It is true that one woman who claimed to have had a very strong emotional bond with her husband who worked on the *Thresher*, insisted at the time that she just 'knew' that her husband was still alive after the 'disaster'. She said that she and her husband had such a spiritual-emotional connection that they always knew when the other was in trouble. Researchers Will Carson and Jeannie Joy interviewed the woman mentioned above shortly after the disappearances. She said:

> My husband was on the submarine *Thresher* when it disappeared. I don't consider myself a widow. I don't believe my husband is dead. No, it's not a matter of just not being able to believe it, to accept reality; I just can't get

over the conviction that he's still alive somewhere. I love my husband very much. I know he loved -- loves me. We were very close. We could always tell when something was wrong with each other. Intuition, I guess. I should have felt something the instant there was trouble, if he was really in serious trouble and knew it -- a matter of life and death -- but I didn't.

What do you believe really happened? Carson and Joy asked the attractive young woman.

Most people think I'm crazy when I say this, but I believe the *Thresher* was captured."

By whom?

I can't say for sure, but there was a Russian submarine spotted near there that day (that is, near where it reportedly vanished 220 miles off Boston harbor) -- only I can't imagine how even the Russians could CAPTURE a vessel like the *Thresher* without leaving the slightest evidence! John J. Williams' source, the retired Navy officer (whose credentials Williams verified), stated that "an eccentric billionaire" (Howard Hughes!?) financed the false *Thresher* "recovery operation" to satisfy the public and the media.

For information on the Navy's investigations of the aqua-labyrinths via nuclear subs, etc., see: "California Floats on Ocean?'" article in the March, 1980 issue of John J. Williams' **Rebel Magazine**.

The **Deros** were beings allegedly tormenting those on the surface of the earth through psychic attack and electronic mind control from their underworld lairs, in preparation for a possible future invasion of the outer world.

In his chapter: 'Old Gold', Lee describes a conversation which he had several years ago with a small group of Death Valley explorers. The conversation turned to the subject of Paihute Indian legends. Two of the men, Jack and Bill, described their experience with an underground city which they claimed to have discovered after one of them had fallen through the bottom of an old mine shaft near Wingate Pass.

They found themselves in a natural underground cavern which they claimed they followed for about 20 miles north into the heart of the Panamint Mountains. To their amazement, they claimed, they found themselves in an huge, ancient, underground cavern city. The 'deeper' underground kingdom of the ancient race who built the city within the Panamints, a civilization that was still alive and thriving after thousands of years. See the Mojave history in Bourke Lee's book '**Death Valley Men**' (MacMillan Co., N.Y. 1932).

This letter is in reply to your January 31 letter. Please forgive me for not answering sooner. Enclosed is some material I hope that you can glean something of value (from). Please be as candid as you have been in the past and if I am far off base don't hesitate to tell me...

Our foundation has located a vast system of underground passages in the Mother Lode country of California. They were first discovered in 1936, ignored by all even with our best efforts to reveal them. Recently a road crew blasted out an opening verifying our claims. ONE (of the chambers is) 200 feet long, 70 feet wide and 50 feet high.

We have disclosed what we believe to be a vast subterranean drainage system (probably traversing the

Great American Desert country for a distance of more than 600 miles). We believe this system extends out like five fingers of your hand to such landmarks as Zion Canyon in Utah, the Grand Canyon, another runs south from the Carson Sink in Nevada and yet another follows (below) the western slope of the same range, joining it's counterpart and ending somewhere in the Mojave Desert.

We believe, contrary to orthodox geologists, that the existence of this underground system drains all surface waters running into Nevada (none, with the exception of the Armagosa runs out) and accounts for the fact that it is a Great American Desert. The hairy creatures that you have written about have been seen in several of these areas. Certainly there has been much 'saucer' activity in these parts. For two years I have collected material pertinent to these creatures and if you have any opinions along these lines I would appreciate hearing them.

So much for now. I hope that I am still your friend. Much of my time has been devoted (to) helping a farmer near Portland who has made a fantastic discovery of incredible stone artifacts. He has several tons of them. They predate anything yet found (or accepted), let us say that for now. We are making slow but steady progress in getting through the wall of orthodoxy. - *Chuck Edwards.*

Linda Moulton-Howe also confirmed the fact that strange aerial disks have often been reported in connection with animal mutilations:

Throughout the history of the animal mutilations since 1967, there have been many eyewitness accounts of

54

large, glowing disks or 'silent helicopters' over pastures where dead animals were later found. One Waco, Texas rancher said he encountered two four-foot tall, light green-colored creatures with large, black, slanted eyes, carrying a calf which was later found dead and mutilated.

In 1983, a Missouri couple watched through binoculars as two small beings in tight-fitting silver suits worked on a cow in a nearby pasture. The alien heads were large and white in color. Nearby, a tall, green-skinned 'lizard man' stood glaring with eyes slit by vertical pupils like a crocodile's....

The indications are that even children are at times utilized for the implementation of plans of these evil powers. That possibility is illustrated by the following incident.

On December 12, 1967, Mrs. Rita Malley was driving along a public highway to her home at Ithaca, New York, with her five- year-old son Dana in the back seat of her vehicle. At about 7:00 P.M. she suddenly realized that a red light was apparently following her, and as she was moving above the speed level, her first reaction was that she was about to be pulled over. She looked through her window and found that it was not a police car behind her but an eerie flying object, moving along above the power lines at the left of her car. Then she found she no longer had control of her vehicle, and shouted to her son to brace himself. However, he remained motionless as though he were in a trance.

A white beam of light flashed down from the vehicle overhead, then she heard voices that sounded weird, broken, and jerky. She herself became hysterical, but through it all her son took no notice whatever of her cries. The radio was not on, but she heard those voices tell her that at that moment a friend of hers had been involved in a terrible accident some miles away. The next day she found that this was indeed true. The voices also told her that her son would not remember anything that had happened. The ordeal was terrifying to Mrs. Malley herself, and for some time afterward whenever she remembered the episode she would break down sobbing.

It would seem possible, then, that pliable children are especially useful for the purposes of these beings. Many children have been used as tools so that men and women would believe in these beings who have a plan whose totality has not yet been revealed.

These incidents are not limited to children. Mrs. Ralph Butler was watching flashing lights outside Owatonna in Minnesota one night in November, 1966. She was with a friend, and suddenly her friend became immobile, with her head dipped down. Mrs. Butler herself heard a voice talking to her, but soon the ordeal was over. However, when the two friends tried to discuss the incident later, both found they immediately suffered blinding headaches. Mrs. Butler also told of hearing strange voices on her radio, and of having peculiar visits from 'air force officers.' This pattern is reported by many who claim to have been contacted by UFO personnel.

The Butler family have experienced various poltergeist phenomena since that 1966 experience -- glass objects moving around and breaking without any known cause, strange noises being heard throughout the house, even telephones and television sets being strangely interfered with.

Researcher David Dobbs of Cincinnati, OH., described the following 'resume of report received... after the MUFON 40-meter net on April, 5, 1980.':

Mike (deleted) from Iowa (deleted) stated that during the period 1961-63 he performed radio maintenance at the atomic proving ground. He also did some top-secret radio work for the Air Force at times. The U-2 was developed here.

Area 51 was located 60 miles due east of the base camp, behind a mountain range separating it from Yucca Flat. Here a secret operation was performed under unbelievable security precautions known as 'Project Redlight.' A UFO which had been shipped from Edwards AFB was flown here. It was not conventionally powered, but was SILENT in operation. Mike assumed that this was the disc recovered intact and shown in the UFO movie reported by radar technicians. Security in Project Red Light was so strict that no one stayed there more than six months. Mike did not see this movie himself, however.

While on vacation, he saw a story in Reader's Digest at his parent's home which told of a UFO exploding over the test site in 1962 while being flown. This would have been a recent story at the time. Mike is aware of the conventionally-powered disc built by the Air Force which was publicized. We both feel that this may have been a cover-up for the real project which he describes. He also heard the stories about parts from a UFO which could not be duplicated successfully by aerospace contractors on the west coast, and many of the rumors about UFOs which have emanated from Nellis AFB. Incidentally, Nellis AFB operated Area 51 where he says the UFO was flown.

This information has bothered him for 20 years, and he wonders if it might be possible for documentation regarding 'Project Red Light' to be obtained under the Freedom of Information Act.

Rod Steiger, longtime UFO & ET investigator, reported the following story:

In 1969 I and my research associates... Loring G. Williams and Glenn McWane, were bombarded with the claims of dozens of contactees who said that they had had an implant left somewhere in their skulls, usually just behind the left ear. These contactees/ abductees came from a wide variety of occupations, cultural backgrounds, and age-groups.

We employed private detectives and medical doctors ... in an attempt to learn what archetype had been fed into their particular group consciousness. We never found any implants that were detectable to X rays, but our hypnotic sessions turned up an incredible number of fascinating, albeit bizarre, stories about underground UFO bases, hybrid A-liens walking among us, and thousands of humans slowly turning into automatons because of readjusted brain wave patterns.

In another story we heard much later from Dagmar and Carl R., they have a farm in northeast Iowa about forty miles from the Mississippi River. One night in August of 1982, Carl observed what he called at the time a 'lantern in the sky' that hovered over him while he was working late in the field...

Two months later in October that year, while Carl was working late in the field preparing for the annual corn harvest, he was startled to see the glowing 'lantern' return to the sky above him. It appeared to be the same object that he had seen in August.

Although he tried to remain oblivious to the object, it seemed to be hovering above him, even following him up and down the corn rows. He became nervous and disconcerted and went back to the farmhouse, where he asked Dagmar to come out and witness the strange object.

Dagmar was able to see the object, too, and they stood and watched it for several minutes before it suddenly moved high into the night sky and then sped off at a great rate of speed in a westerly direction.

About three the next morning, Carl was awakened by the sound of cattle bellowing nervously in the stockyard. As he got out of bed and looked out the bedroom window, he saw a disk-shaped object hovering above the barnyard. It was glowing in a kind of greenish color...

Following this, the couple was 'tranquilized' by the object or its occupants somehow, possibly by some kind of intoxicating, pacifying or STIM-ulating ray which apparently induced a drugged or trance-like electrochemical reaction in their brains and bodies, after which they were taken somewhere by some entities where a conventional 'abduction' sequence followed, similar to those described by so many others.

Steiger related the couples' after-thoughts concerning their abduction by 'smallish' large-eyed beings "with only nostril openings (rather than a pronounced nose) and with tight, expressionless lips.

Steiger continues:

While the young Iowa couple can remember no further UFO interaction since that particular autumn, they both admit to being nervous about having another encounter. Carl, especially, feels that he was used. Dagmar speculated that bits of her skin tissue might have been removed in the examination, and although she does not claim to be an expert in such matters, she wonders if enough of her body could be cloned in a way to interact with whatever embryo or fetus might have been fathered by the semen that was taken from her husband (Note: Dagmar claimed that during one part of the 'examination' a needle-like object was stuck into her abdomen. Many believe that this is one process by which the 'entities' extract ovum from human females - *Branton*).

Not wanting to sound like victims of some science fiction thriller, the young couple have theorized that they might have been used in some strange program of creating hybrid beings. Perhaps, they suggest, Carl's semen was used to impregnate an alien female or an Earth female, who is somehow influenced by and under the control of alien beings. In either event, they are uncomfortable with the experience and with the memory of the encounter. Both of them feel as though they may have been used in ways opposed to their normal expression of will.

Dagmar has gone even farther in her speculations by suggesting that if bits of her body could have been used to create a clone and if Carl's semen could somehow be used at a future time to impregnate such a clone, then alien beings could be breeding their own brand of humans as part of an organized program to create an army of human-like robots that would be totally under control of A-liens in their master plan to conquer Earth.

DEALS & TREATIES WITH ET's

During the period 1969-1971, MJ-12 representing the U.S. Government made a deal with these creatures, called EBE's [Extra-terrestrial Biological Entities, named by Detley Bronk, original MJ-12 member and 6th President of John Hopkins University]. The 'deal' was that in exchange for technology ' that they would provide to us, we agreed to ignore the abductions that were going on and suppress information on the cattle mutilations. The EBE's assured MJ-12 that the abductions [usually lasting about 2 hours] were merely the ongoing monitoring of developing civilizations.

Cattle mutilations that were prevalent throughout the period from 1973 to 1983 and publicly noted through news-paper and magazine stories and included a documentary produced by Linda Howe for a Denver CBS affiliate KMGH-TV, were for the collection of these tissues by the A-liens. Mutilations comprised removal of genitals, rectums cored out to the colon, eyes, tongue, and throat all surgically removed with extreme precision. In some cases the incis-ions were made by cutting between the cells, a process we are not yet capable of performing in the field. In many of the

61

mutilations there was no blood ound at all in the carcass, yet there was no vascular collapse of the internal organs.

• In fact, the procedure for an abduction turned out to be: "The insertion of a 3mm spherical device through the nasal cavity of the abductee into the brain [optic and/or nerve center], the device is used for the biological monitoring, tracking, and control of the abductee.

• Implementation of Post-hypnotic Suggestions to carry out specific activities during a specific time period, the actuation of which occurred within the next 2 to 5 years.

• *Termination of some people so that they could function as living sources for biological material and substances.*

• *Termination of individuals who represent a threat to the continuation of their activity.*

• *Effect genetic engineering experiments. Impregnation of Human females and early termination of pregnancies to secure the crossbreed infant.* (Note: Or perhaps a better term for it would be a "genetically altered" infant, since there has been no evidence forthcoming that an actual hybrid between Humans and EBE or Grey species have been successful.

One source, an Area 51 worker-member of a secret Naval Intelligence group called COM-12 by the name of Michael Younger, stated that the Bavarian Black Nobility [secret societies] have agreed to turn over three-quarters of the planet to the Greys if they could retain 25 percent for themselves and have access to Alien mind-control technology.

62

A-liens would assist in the abduction, programming and implanting of people throughout the world in preparation for a New World Order -- which in turn would be annexed to the Alien empire. Apparently some top-echelon Bavarians have agreed to this, since they realize that they NEED the Alien mind-control and implant technology in order to carry out their plans for world domination. (NOTE: Although Dan Burisch states that the Tau-9 Treaty with EBES is being negotiated, he gives none of the stipulations, terms or conditions; however, the on-line copy does not refer to any "rights"--not human, not natural, not lawful.

In the present atmosphere of Human intimidation and genocide, I postu-late that the above paragraph must indeed articulate the conditions long time as part of their agenda to implement absolute electronic control over the inhabitants of planet earth. which the Tau-9 Treaty will force on our Planet's peoples, except if Divine Intervention, natural forces, other parties get involved. We the people are toast, cattle, chattel and slaves to a New World Order system that literally reverts Humanity back to medieval means and methods-- thanks to MJ12 never having told us all the Truth.)

SECTION 5: THE 1970s

Reptile "people" have always been encountered in deep underground installations below the Mojave Desert region of California... and even on the fringe of the desert itself near Lancaster and elsewhere. In many cases they have been seen working closely with the Greys, which regard these Reptons or Lizard Men as being their superiors.

It is remarkable that the majority of the non-human occupants which are reported in connection with these aerial craft are said to be Reptoid or Saurian in nature, especially in light of such prophecies as the one given in Revelation chapter 12, which reads:

... And there was WAR IN HEAVEN: Michael fought against THE DRAGON; and THE DRAGON fought and his angels... and the GREAT DRAGON was cast out, that OLD SERPENT, called the Devil, and Satan, which DECIEVETH the whole world.."

Callers to the Billy Goodman Radio Happening had already organized trips to mile-marker 29 1/2 on highway

375 where a dirt road left the highway to intersect the road to Dreamland. There was a heavy black mail box on this road which identified it. I got to Rachel early one October morning and left my card with Pat at Rachel's Bar and Grill to pass on to Yellow Fruit. She knew him by sight. I then inspected the dirt roads where people stood to observe the test flights.

I had already interviewed four witnesses by phone who testified that they had seen UFOs over the Groom Mountains on certain nights in the same area they were seen by John Lear. I made a second trip to the area in late October where a public group visited Rachel and that is when I saw the mysterious Yellow Fruit in the cafe. He later called me on the phone. I left him with a copy of my book, 'Alien Magic' and he remarked on the research I had done concerning the search for underground bases.

According to YellowFruit and others there are underground bases and tunnels that conceal activities of A-liens and secret government projects... The following is an excerpt from an article which appeared in a UFO-related publication. We do not know exactly who the author of the article is, but we relate the excerpt as it was sent to us:

...Lear directed my attention to a large map of Nevada, which delineates all the areas which civilian maps coyly leave as uncharted military preserves. 'Right in the very center is a place called Area 51. It is our most secret complex. There are 1900 people there -- it takes presidential clearance to work there -- and they're ferried in by aircraft in the morning and taken out about 5 o'clock in the evening. They have nothing to do with the saucers.

The people who work on the saucers go up later in the afternoon, and go home about midnight. The saucer facility is called S-4.' S-4 is in the southwest corner of Area 51.

Unfortunately, this facility -- and a similar set-up near Dulce, New Mexico -- may now belong to forces not loyal to the U.S. Government, or even the human race. 'It's horrifying for us to think that all the scientists we think are working for us are actually controlled by the A-liens.'

Here, Lear seems to contradict himself. He speaks of 'A-liens,' plural, in a controlling capacity, whereas previously he noted but one survivor, kept as captive. He resolves this conflict by describing an alleged landing at Holloman Air Force Base on April 24, 1964 -- our first diplomatic contact, as it were, with the visitors

(Note: In addition, this writer does not take into account the apparent subterranean connection and origin of many of the 'alien' beings, which has been alleged by many sources and which WOULD explain the large alien influence or presence in Nevada and elsewhere - Branton). According to Lear and other sources, the 1973 Robert Emenegger documentary '*UFOS: Past, Present & Future*' presented a thinly-fictionalized version of this event; government contacts allegedly provided the film-makers actual footage of the meeting, which, alas, was withdrawn at the last moment for as-yet un-specified reasons.

A deal was made with them in the latter part of the 1960s (Note: As we've indicated earlier, this might have been a 'revisioning' of an earlier treaty, as certain sources claim that these treaties go back to the 1930's, if not earlier. Some of those involved in this 'deal' may have had good intentions, since the Greys presented themselves as evolved 'space brothers' who only wanted to help us.

John Lear even alleged that huge underground bases were constructed with the 'help' of the Greys, yet when completed, the Greys did an about face and took control of not only the lower levels of these bases but also the mechanisms which were supposedly given to the government as part of the deal. This is about the time that the 'wars' began within the subterranean system itself, near the time when the so- called Grand Deception of the A-liens was discovered --*Branton.*

In exchange for technology, we would cover up the existence of the A-liens.' Apparently this agreement, engineered by an arm of government so covert that even the President may not be on the 'need to know' list -- also sanctioned the abduction of humans, which the A-liens rationalized as an ongoing monitoring of a developing civilization. We asked only for a list of the abductees.

In 1973, the deal soured. Hundreds of people-- thousands—were being abducted that weren't on the list. In 1978-79, there was an altercation between us and the A-liens, in which they killed 44 of our top scientists, and a number of Delta forces who were trying to free them. I'm not sure where this altercation occurred -- it could have been Dulce (probably Dulce, as the term 'Dulce Wars' -- which has been referred to by different sources -- would seem to indicate. Also, there is some confusion as to the "66" and "44" numbers.

ABDUCTIONS Come to Light.--

UFO investigator Richard Siefried was told by Pam Owens that she was taken aboard a UFO on November 25, 1978, while she was expecting a child. She was nineteen at the time, and she had no memory of the abduction until she was hypnotically regressed. Then she was able to give full and fascinating details of her encounter.

Mrs. Owens told Siefried that she was paralyzed and able to move only her eyes. She lay helpless on a table and stared up in terror at two weird-looking creatures.

According to Mrs. Owens, their heads were hairless, oversize domes, their eyes were big and sunk back in their skulls. The greenish skin covering their bodies was coarse. Each hand had four fingers that she described as being twice as long as humans'. And to her terror, one of those strange hands was holding a long silver needle, preparing to plunge it into her stomach...

Paul Bennewitz says that 66 Special Forces were killed in an attempt to set free some of our scientists from the "A-liens" that had taken them captive, whereas 44 escaped. Whether the 44 were storm-troopers or scientists is uncertain, although most sources state that the scientist did NOT make it out alive. Bennewitz claims that the "44" did not die but escaped instead. Since some report that the scientists were NOT set free it may have been that 100 special forces were sent in -- 66 of them being killed in the attempt and 44 escaping the alien counter-attack - Branton), or it could have occurred in Groom Lake (Robert Lazar has stated that a similar confrontation between the A-liens and human Security DID occur in the bases below Groom Lake -

Branton.) Phil Schneider's story confirms Bennewitz' and Branton's; but all three are done, dead and gone.

[And that's why I'm sitting here doing this compilation—because Corporate Silicon Valley executives Bezos and Zuckerberg are censoring and suppressing information about these matters in social media. On my web-site, www.abidemiracles.com, thirty-seven video titles concerning UFOs, ET's, Abductions and Underground Facilities—the issue of Human Rights vs. Treaties—were censored and removed from my LINKS section, in the name of social media political-correctness.--*Editor*]

This 1979 battle between the Greys, Saurians and us Humans, Lear concludes leaves us bereft of "our own" facilities underground. And ever since, we have attempted to create a counterforce to meet the alien challenge." (In other words, the 'A-liens' invaded and took control of the underground bases -- probably from BELOW -- and killed many of our top scientists, destroying much of 'our' ability to defend ourselves, at least technically, from their ongoing incursions - *Branton*)

The following information from William F. Hamilton III appeared in **"*UFO Universe*"** and describes further details on the 'Yellow Fruit' account, including claims which YF made over the air during the few 'interviews' in which he took part on KVEG Radio's Billy Goodman talk show:

> Yellow Fruit revealed that a conflict is still going on between benevolent ET's versus Saurian & Grey EBE's, and that now we can only hope the benevolent ones have gained the upper hand at Dreamland where he said a

69

contingent of 37 benevolent ones were stationed and where 3 EBE's were held in captivity.

The Strategic Defense Initiative was one such scheme. 'SDI, regardless of what you hear, was completed two years ago; that was to shoot down incoming saucers. The mistake was that we thought they were coming inbound - in fact, they're already here. They're in underground bases all over the place.' It seems that the A-liens had constructed many such bases without our knowledge, where they conduct heinous genetic experiments on animals, human beings, and 'improvised' creatures of their own devising.'"

Researcher Jim Bennett, in a letter to Jacques Vallee dated Jan. 15, 1992, made some startling disclosures in regards to the Alien situation and the Dulce, N.M. base in particular. It is my belief that even if there is a fascist-CIA cabal trying to establish a world dictatorship using the 'threat' of an Alien invasion to foment world government, that the 'threat' may be real all the same. It is also possible that the Bavarians may be working with very *real* A-liens in an end-game designed to establish a world government using this 'threat' as an excuse to do so, although when the world is under 'their' control the Illuminati may betray the Human race by turning much of the global government control-system over to the Grey A-liens [the Beast?].

The A-liens may have been collaborating with the Bavarians for an extended period of time, based on the content of the Greada Treaty Eisenhower signed. In his lengthy letter, Jim Bennett, director of the research organization '**Planet.com**', writes:

70

[The year] 1947 brought the passage of the National Security Act, the start of the NAZI germinated CIA and NSA. The influx of at least a hundred Nazi scientists, engineers, etc., into the United States and Canada. –

(**Note**: Other sources claim that eventually over 3000 Nazi S.S. agents entered the U.S. under Operation Paperclip in this manner--not just former Nazis but active Nazi SS's who still maintained national socialist philosophy and agendas they carried on to a planned conclusion—New World Order.

They were given refuge within the military-industrial complex with the help of members of the Bavarian-based black gnostic -- serpent worshiping Lodges in America such as the Jesuit-spawned Scottish Rite and related lodges, who control oil-military-industrial complex. Leadership of the Military-Industrial Complex or M.I.C. not only gave these Fascists refuge following the war, but also financed the Nazi war machine itself during the second world war. - *Branton*).

A Nazi aeronautical engineer, a certain Herr Mieth -- who designed four different types of saucer- shaped craft by 1943 using either rocket power or donut configuration jet turbine engines, with the cabin stabilized by gyro, the compressors rotating in one direction and the expansion chambers and vectored exhausts rotating in the opposite direction -- was traced to Canada in 1947 and began work for the A.V.Roe company [Avroe disk]. The phony AVROE 'aircar' was definitely to disinform the press as to the real projects underway underground in Canada.

An eight mile long train that went out of Austria in 1945 [672 traincars!], to the coast of Brittany, the contents loaded on board ships, eventually ending up underground in Southwestern Canada. At the same time over 100 prefab factory buildings were shipped from England to British Columbia. ... the Nazis had everything before any other country, they had radar in 1933, they had infra-red sensors, heavy water, etc., etc.

(NOTE: Know WHY the Nazis got all this? Because their way of Elitist race-culling is common to the Annunaki Race, technologically superior, physically stronger than Greys, who come from the Sirius system. The way was prepared telepathically by Bavarians and the Theosophy movement, for eugenics control of populations through financial endowments of and by the Rockefeller Foundation on the false accusation that this planet is over-populated, which is isn't and never was.)

We have been told lie after lie in terms of who invented these things. If anyone in the world had access to 'Alien' technology it was the Aryans [Nazis]. Only because their metallurgy and casting were flawed, or they would have succeeded in conquering the world.

As you probably know, many expatriate Nazis were given carte blanche--new IDs--and were included in [the] startup of more than several departments of the CIA in 1947, Departments including 'genetics and cloning' [with some of the same 'doctors' who had given death camp residents gangrene, etc.] 'designer drugs and mind control' using the same scientists who had developed the drugs Methadone and Methedrine for Hitler.

(But in 1952, a public stir caused the CIA to shuffle these fab fellows out of town. My guess is to various underground centers that were being built. "...I have talked to Paul Bennewitz at length, several times."]

Paul Bennewitz, a pilot, flew over the Dulce area numerous times on his way between Albuquerque and Denver. He took many pictures of the construction going on, and according to Paul, he also took pictures of circular craft on the ground at this site which, as late as 1973 according to him, had large hanger doors much the same as Lazar's second hand explanation about the doors at S-4. [All the stuff from Area 51 and 'S-4' having to do with inertial mass cancellation was moved to an area near St. George Utah.] The most revealing photos and their negatives disappeared in about 1975 when various 'fringe UFO experts' visited Paul.

Also, his house was burglarized and ransacked more than once. In later years Moore, Shandera, and Torme made a meaningless tour of Dulce when they went on to Albuquerque [the real reason for their travels] to see if there was any more evidence of serious consequence still in Paul's possession that they could grab; and sure enough, he was missing some photos when they left his house. If you even talked to Bennewitz, you would have gotten a lot closer to having a 'revelation'...

The 'waste' from the underground bio-genetic lab comes out in the river canyon about ten miles below Navajo Dam-- (Reptiloid grey A-liens are involved – as well as biogenetically-constructed beings developed by Illuminati-Thule-CIA-backed scientists working in the Dulce facility -

73

Branton) – although these days they 'treat it' a lot more before letting their 'grey'-water back into the environment. This base and others are of course connected by tunnels to Los Alamos. The Archuleta Mesa installation rivals Pine Gap at Alice Springs, Australia for security, etc. Every U.S. Air Force base has a so-called 'bolt-hole' and is connected to this bolt-hole by tunnel...

History testifies, following World War II over 2,000 German 'immigrants' to the U.S. became members of the American Psychiatric Association, which was involved in GUN CONTROL lobbying. In light the collaboration between Bavarian Thule Society and the Bavarian Illuminati and the influx of Thule-backed fifth-column Nazi SS agents into U.S. Intell--with the help of Illuminati-backed Oil barrens like the German-immigrant Aryan-supremacist Rockefellers and their corporate oil-chemical empires [**Exxon, Arco, Zapata**, etc.].

In light of the deadly intent of Bavarian societies to establish a New World Order--as Adolph Hitler laid out in his second book, **The New World Order**—one has to wonder WHY so many German nationals join an association that dealt directly with the study of people's minds.

This is not to say that Germans themselves are to blame, it is rather, German-Bavarian Fascists are behind the New World Order agenda, and especially the Satanist Germanic Black Nobility families who claim direct descent from the early leaders of the [un]Holy Roman Empire of Germany that rose from a remnant of the Roman Empire and kept Europe in an iron grip throughout the Dark Ages.

These were the "13 families" who had ruled vast financial empires in Europe for nearly 1500 years. They are once again taking control of the world as they attempted to do with World Wars I and II, provoke a global war that will result in the massive 'de-population' of Blacks, Asians, Jews, Slavs, and many others -- excepting of course for the 'Aryan elite' class. In essence, they intend to finish what Adolph Hitler set out to accomplish. The threat then is from 'Nazism' or National 'Socialism', whether it be European, British or American or whether it be political, corporate or occult National Socialism.

As in situations arising in Vietnam and Korea, wherein Socialist leaders of the United Nations Organization were playing both sides of the chessboard, a war waged by the "New World Order" against Grays will no doubt be a no-win conflict that will only serve to reduce population of the planet, which is after all, part and parcel of the overall Draconian-Bavarian global agenda.

Another possibility that has been suggested is that the Grays will be made out to be the good guys who need 'our' help to break free from the tall Reptiloids and their empire that had conquered them in the past, or visa versa. Actually the collaboration between Reptiloids and Grays has been undertaken with the full consent of both sides, and behind the scenes collectivist Reptiloids, Insectoids, Grays and Bavarian secret society lodges are all working together.

Many scenarios are possible... however the important thing to remember is that ANY war waged against the Reptilian Grays that threatens the American Declaration of Independence, U.S. Constitution and the Bill of Rights is merely playing into the hands of A-liens, either way you look at it. All one has to do is look at the Treaties. They are commercial, Maritime-Admiralty, Uniform Commercial Code, Administrative Statutes in which **NO HUMAN RIGHTS EXIST, BY DEFINITIONS.**

International cooperation in common defense against Alien threat is one thing; but overthrow of Common Law of the Lands is quite another, aided and abetted by a Legal Profession dominated and manipulated by ideologies—Zionist, Islamist and Globalist. National Sovereignty is the tip of this iceberg. The real threat is the interstellar and galactic practice of commercial human-trafficking in the following formats, sanctioned by these Commercial Treaties:

1. Sexual slavery and human trafficking of children and young women;

2. Trafficking of non-violent "dissident felons" into for-profit prisons—whether debtor-prisons, reform schools or detention centers;

3, Body-parts marketing by hospitals and Planned Parenthood, and "soul trafficking" by predatory ET's.4. Social Services' trafficking of children removed from the home due to trivial and non-essential charges: refusal of vaccinations, use of "weed," herbs and/or homeopathic remedies, home schooling or dissident activities.

4. Drug- and gun-running, international sale of DU armaments weapons of mass destruction and uranium to fuel wars. Not one of these above activities can be construed

as a matter of national ***defense***--only of "offense" and/or
piracy and violations of human and natural rights.

In this world, those who control the money control
governments by controlling what Laws get enforced, by
whom and how. Independent economies are what prevent all
nations from falling like dominoes if an economic collapse is
staged and made to occur; therefore national autonomy,
regional problem-solving and human dominions must be
respected by Laws of the Land, which at this time favor
industry and penalize human life everywhich way. (Notice
the typical Annunaki—non-Human—craft below.)

SECTION 6: THE 1980s

Dr. Roger Lier, M.D. removed ET-implants from abductees until he himself was taken out covertly and suddenly, age 67.

Physical Implants: Artifacts of Technology

I-the-Editor of this anthology personally had a childhood abduction experience in 1953 when I was nine during a vacation to Minnesota with my foster mother. We were staying at a cabin by a lake, and I walked out before breakfast from the cabin to the lake at 9am, got in a canoe that was tied up at the dock that belonged to the family we were visiting, and I rowed out . . . Twelve hours later, I returned . . . and everybody was white-faced. Nobody said a word or asked why I did that.

For more than ten years afterward, I suffered from fainting spells at random, with no known cause; and eventually, half a century later, two implants popped out that had affected my nervous system physically and my attitude behaviorally, as I lived an abstracted and distant state. When I finally held actual physical implants—metal covered in-- plastic—in my hand, the memories about the abduction itself and the horror of it surfaced; so I suppress those memories. But I still have one more implant behind my right ear.

Bill Hamilton reports, on Implant Devices:

"...Alien vehicles are being tested at the alien physical technology center at S-4 at the Nevada Test Site. Alien vehicles are being replicated at Kirtland AFB & Sandia Laboratories & these replicas are referred to as ARVs (Alien Reproductive Vehicles). At least three of these vehicles are stored in hangers at Norton AFB, California. ... It is alleged that vehicle propulsion units were constructed by General Electric & composite materials were provided by Amoco. Alien vehicles generate an artificial gravity field which can be focused & intensified for high speed travel...

Alien organisms and biological technology are tested (in the upper levels - *Branton*) at the underground biogenetic laboratories at Dulce, New Mexico. Alien genetic engineering, cloning, & cryogenic technology have been studied with a view towards 'enhancing' human genetics, deciphering the human genome, & gaining a biological advantage by artificial biological engineering. Strange life forms have been bred in these laboratories.

Racial Characteristics as a Weapon-of-Choice

The analysis of ET-devices by technical staff has produced a description that involves use of crystalline technology combined with molecular circuitry and these ride on the resonant emissions of the brain and the various fields of the human (body). Information is entrained on the brain waves. It appears that all attempts to remove the implants

(1972) have resulted in the death of the human. They perform surgery and other operations on human subjects. These abductions continue to be an ongoing matter. A list of abductees [presumably was] provided periodically to MAJI, although it [was] known that many more are abducted than are reported... Various descriptions of the ALF's relate the following characteristics:

Between 3 to 5 feet in height, erect standing biped, small thin build, head larger than humans, absence of auditory lobes (external), absence of body hair, large... eyes (slanted approximately 35 degrees) which are opaque black with vertical slit pupils, arms resembling praying mantis (normal attitude) which reach to the knees, long hands with small palm, claw-like fingers (various number of digits - often two short digits and two long, but some species have three or four fingers), tough gray skin which is Reptoid in texture, small feet with four small claw-like toes... a non-functioning digestive system; The two separate brains are separated by mid-cranial lateral bone (anterior and posterior brain). There is no apparent connection between the two (could one be an 'individual' brain while the other works as part of a 'collective consciousness'? - *Branton*) movement is deliberate, slow and precise.

Many details of ET-humanoids are actually similar to all branches of the Reptoid race as described by other witnesses. It appears as if serpent Race is composed of several different branches or types, much the same as dogs and other animals retain their distinction but are composed of several different types or breeds.

The U.S. Government was NOT initially aware of the far reaching consequences of their 'deal'. They were led to believe that abductions were essentially benign, and since they figured that the abductions would probably go on anyway whether they agreed or not, they merely insisted on a current list of abductees be submitted on a periodic basis to MJ-12 and the National Security Council.

*Does this sound incredible? An actual list of abductees sent to the National Security Council? Then—***We abductees in the early years are on that list**. Read on, because there's more.

EBE's have a genetic disorder in that their digestive system is atrophied and not functional... In order to sustain themselves they use enzyme or hormonal secretions obtained from tissues that they extract from Humans and animals. Secretions obtained are then mixed with hydrogen peroxide [to kill germs, viruses, etc.] and applied on the skin by spreading or dipping parts of their bodies in the solution. The body absorbs the solution, then excretes the waste back through the skin. Urine is also excreted through the skin in this manner, which may explain the ammonia-like stench that many abductees or witnesses have reported [Preston Nichol's 1983 description of Reptoids serving in the Montauk Project is particularly entertaining.--*Editor*] during encounters with the grey-type A-liens. - *Branton*).

Alien substance requires that they must have human blood and other biological substances to survive. In extreme circumstances they can subsist on other (cattle, etc.) animal fluids. Food is converted to energy by Chlorophyll, by a photosynthetic process (this supports results gained from

81

autopsies at 29 Palms underground base where it was seen that their 'blood' was greenish and the tissue was black).

Waste products are secreted through the skin. . Some autopsies have revealed a crystalline network which is thought to have a function in telepathic (and other) functions which help to maintain the group consciousness between members of the same species. Functions of group consciousness in this species does have a disadvantage in that decisions in this species comes rather slowly as the matter at hand filters through the group awareness of those who must make the decision . . .

There is one reported case where a worker at the Dougway Test Site claimed to have seen a man temporarily transform into a Reptoid while he was changing a tire, but the most interesting case was that of a woman, Barbara, who worked in the small town of Dougway as a hair dresser. She worked on many of the base personnel there. On one occasion a customer who was a high- ranking military officer at the base came in. While she was working on his 'hair', she noticed a brief transformation during which she saw the officer turn into a Reptoid creature.

K.S., a Salt Lake City based UFOlogist, claims that during an Open Mind UFO gathering in the early 1990's, Barbara alleged that while working at Dougway she heard rumors that Reptoid humanoids were operating all over the base.

Another former Dougway worker, Ray White, who was a top secret courier, stated that during his work at the base [1970's?] he witnessed an experiment where an object was teleported from one room to another. He also noticed that high-ranking Russian officers sometimes visited the base. He also claimed that some of the people that he met there were NOT human. When asked what he thought they were, he did not know, but he did mention that top secret research into advanced robotics was being carried out at the base - *Branton*)

A U.S. Intelligence worker (O.S.I.) by the name of 'Tucker', a Security Officer at the Test Site who had called in to the Billy Goodman talk show (KVEG radio - Las Vegas, NV) on a few occasions, used the codename: 'Yellowfruit,' writing to John Lear. (who is one of the most decorated test pilots in U.S. history, and whose father William Lear founded Lear Jet Corp., invented the 8-track tape recorder, and so on) who himself claims many connections with people 'in the know'.

The codename "Yellowfruit" belongs to a top secret group that worked at the site, with which Tucker was involved who also sent Lear a copy of the 'Benevolents' teachings. The 'Benevolents' are allegedly working at the Test Site with MJ-12 who are 'Blond-Nordic and/or Aryan-like' people.

QUOTE John Lear--

" . . . There is a triangle surrounding the Nevada Test Site. There are in fact two of them. Each one frontiers on the other. One is the electro-magnetic triangle, installed by MJ-12. This is a shield to protect the 'Benevolents' (very human looking) from the EBEs (so-called "extraterrestrial biological entities" or Greys - *Branton*) while they help us develop our counter-attack/defenses. The other is the EBEs' 'trap' keeping the benevolents in the redoubt... At each corner of the EM Triangle you will find BLM stations and they are the transmitters of the shield.

"We are like the Chinese, we can't out-tech but we can still out- number them. Especially since they can't breed naturally here, and it is too far for them to go back home without our help. Many of our EM Triangles are ruses to keep them over extended. They can't get out of our solar system because our electro-magnetic field is the wrong frequency for their propulsion system to work efficiently. This explains why the EBEs cannot commit more vehicles to our solar system." . . .

We personally do not believe in 'standoffs'. In war there is no neutrality, one is either attacking (in various ways) or being attacked, in various ways—ways which those on the defensive might not even be aware of. The letter continued:

One headquarter of this particular Thought Group was/is Deep Springs, California. At this location one could find a school' for Communist homosexuals who defected to the EBEs in exchange for a cure for AIDs and a promise of their own little world, including reproduction via cloning and artificial wombs. Their sperm to fertilize eggs were taken from abductees.

You will not likely see the hybrids hidden inside the mountain unless you have ... starlite binoculars. Some homo-saphien-appearing malevolents (*mercenaries*) are also there. Nine Soviets were there at the same time Soviets were at the NTS. They were there in the hopes of talking them into defecting back to our side. We are still hopeful.

Collaborators have used the cover organization called *Natural Resources Defense Council*, with front offices in New York and 1350 New York Avenue, N.W., suite 300, Washington, D.C. 20005. It is headed by Tom Cochran, staffed by Kevin Priestly UNR, John Brune UNR, Holly Eisler UnSan Diego, Gary Reisling Univ. Ca. Pasadena, Holly Nelson NY, Mary Manning LV Sun, Ed Vogel LVR; and many others I can reveal later.

One will also find that each corner of their triangle is at the base of a mountain. At each location you will find several entrances to underground systems. Do not attempt to enter, unless you wish to become liquid protein. But EBEs are allergic to high concentrations of sugar.

Further, According to the letter, both the Nevada Test Site and Deep Springs are areas of conflict between U.S. Govt.-'Nordic' groups who *are at war against* Saurian Grey Reptoids – over the issue and practice of genetic alterations, since the internal physiology of Greys is reportedly Reptoid-based rather than Mammalian-based.

Jason Bishop also released other information he received by way of John Lear, from this individual whose letter we just quoted. which he claimed was not certain whether these 'A-liens' are tied in with the so-called exterran Nordic' Pleiadeans, the terran 'Aryan' Antarcticans, or the subterran 'Blond' Telosians - as all three groups allegedly exist according to different sources, and may have been confused with each other in the past. All three of these groups allegedly posses aerial disks, although in reality their societies may be somewhat distinct from each other.

"Yellowfruit" also provided coordinates for Electromagnetic Triangles he referred to in his letter. These include: N 37 22 30 - E 117 58 0; N 38 21 0 - E 115 35 0; N 35 39 0 - E 114 51 0. Also: Yucca Lake: N 37 0 30 - E 116 7 0.

Bill English, son of an Arizona state legislator and a former Green Beret commander viewed the top-secret document, *"GRUDGE/ Blue Book Report No. 13."* years after he investigated a downed aircraft which radioed an encounter with a UFO, and whose occupants were later found mutilated. He stated that this secret document contained eyewitness descriptions of children who had been abducted by 'Grey' type entities, one of them being abducted on a farm right in front of the parents, and never seen again.

From what we can gather from the letter quoted earlier there are many areas of conflict or standoff between humans and Saurians around the world. Those who realize that the conflict exists, such as the inner government, have failed to warn the general population of the problem possibly out of fear. However, as we have seen, documentation proving that such a hidden conflict between the human and serpent races exists since ancient times is surfacing *en masse*.

As we've indicated, there are numerous accounts suggesting that an ancient race who utilize high-technology now resides in the bowels of Mt. Shasta in the Cascade Range of northern California. According to researcher William F. ["Bill"] Hamilton, who claims to have met representatives of this society, the inhabitants of the subterranean city under Mt. Shasta are usually tall, blue- eyed blonds who number in excess of over one-and-a-half million in their large 5-leveled, 20-mile long underground city.

Mt. Shasta has been a major site for UFO contacts for decades. Also Indian legends - as well as stories of strange people being seen on it's slopes - abound there. These accounts are so well-known that many of the travel guides to the Shasta area mention the legends of the ancient people who are said to dwell within this ancient volcanic peak.

One video we tape we have acquired is an interview with an EBE. Since EBE's communicate telepathically (via psionic crystalline transceiver-like implants that link the Grays together into a mass collective-hive-mind - *Branton*), an Air Force Colonel serves as interpreter.

Just before the recent stock market correction in October of 1987, several newsmen, including Bill Moore, had been invited to Washington D.C., to personally film the EBE in a similar type interview, and distribute the film to the public. Apparently, because of the cor- rection in the market, it was felt the timing was not propitious. In any case, it certainly seems like an odd method to inform the public of extra-terrestrials, but it would be in keeping with the actions of a panicked organization who at this point in time doesn't know which way to turn.

ABDUCTIONS

John Lear claims in his 'Press Release' of June 3, 1988, in reference to human abductees and victims of human mutilation:

Various parts of the body are taken to various underground laboratories, one of which is known to be near the small New Mexico town of Dulce. This jointly occupied (CIA-Alien) facility has been described as enormous, with huge tiled walls that 'go on forever'. Witnesses have reported huge vats filled with amber liquid with parts of human bodies being stirred inside... he secretions obtained are then mixed with hydrogen peroxide and applied on the skin (of the Greys) by spreading or dipping parts of their bodies in the solution. The body absorbs the solution, then excretes the waste back through the skin."

Researcher William Cooper, formerly a chief Petty Officer and Intelligence Worker in the Pacific Naval fleet, pointed out at the 1989 MUFON Conference in Las Vegas that over 3000 children disappear without a trace yearly in one part of Manhattan alone. Manhattan literally sits atop vast underground caverns including CON EDISON at a depth of 200 feet. He also claimed to have seen top-secret reports stating that sections of human bodies were found stored on disks retrieved from crash-recovery sites, and that the government was extremely disturbed by this aspect of the alien activity.

The following information was sent to us via a researcher who is investigating a continuous abduction of a young (at the time) nine-year-old boy in southern Nevada, who may have been taken to underground levels below that same area. Names, addresses and other details have been deleted on request to protect the privacy of the sources. We quote from a series of notes based on the young boys' experiences, exactly as they were sent to a member of "the Group", with our emphasis added:

1: The Greys, he says they don't use words but communicate through him. They show their dis- pleasure by wrinkling their noses and pursing their lips with a slight hissing sound at him.

2: He says he feels like he's being watched wherever he goes (Note: This is a very common observation made by people who claim to have experienced aerial AND/OR subsurface abductions or encounters with non- human A- liens - *Branton*).

3: This is what they look like to him (drawings were included depicting a traditional 'gray' with a somewhat 'wiry' build - *Branton*). This is what the uniform they wear looks like to him. He says the box in the middle has different colored flashing buttons. This is the large 'boat'--a sort of floating island he was brought to (Note: Some aspects of the abduction suggest that the young boy was taken to a large network of water-filled subterranean caverns - *Branton*). There were many 'hybrids' on it also.

4: These were the hybrids he saw. He says that they sit in a large circle holding hands. There is one small candle with a very large flame going. He says he is not afraid of the hybrids. It appears that ET-abductors are extremely cautious and cunning, and have hidden their tracks and even their very existence well, at least up until the 1970's-1980's when abductions started to make the news in a profound way.

Although many of the children who are allegedly abducted and never seen again are of the homeless or unwanted type, street-children of prostitutes, and so on -- children who will not be missed as much as others -- it also appears that thousands of children who belong to middle-class families are also being abducted, implanted and returned. Since the disappearance of these would cause far more 'waves' than a child without a guardian, they are used instead for purposes of manipulation.

Reptoids can inject or encodify a human embryo with Reptoid DNA during the early stages of development. Also, aside from the description given by Dale Russell to the effect that the ancient progenitors of the gray-type Saurians may have had a type of 'ear', we presently know of only one other account describing a possible 'ear-like' appendage having been seen on a Sauroid creature. This was described by a Mr. Brian Scott, who was allegedly abducted into an underground base beneath the Superstition Mts. area east of Phoenix, Arizona. He described these large, fearful creatures as having a type of 'flap' of leathery or 'crocodilian' texture which came down each side of their heads. It is uncertain however whether this was a type of ear-like appendage or not.

These people according to Scott claimed to have a base in 'Epsilon Bootes' and worked with a smaller group of grayish white dwarfs of typical Grey description as well as with a group of 'transparent' entities who referred to themselves as 'the hosts', or the 'Ashtar' beings. As for the so-called hybrids--

Bill Hamilton's testimony seem to be confirmed by others, including abductees, who have hinted that the 'hybrid' fetuses are actually conceived through human spermatozoa taken from men and ovum taken from women abductees, and that the fetuses are as we have stated somehow genetically altered with possible Reptoid 'cells' or genetic coding being added. (Many of the so-called hybrids however are nevertheless 'human', possessing human souls, and human blood—unless they were artificially inseminated, in which case, no Soul ignited at conception - *Branton*).

There are hundreds, if not thousands, of accounts of women who had been a few months along in a pregnancy, most often an unexplained pregnancy, only to find after a UFO abduction experience that their babies suddenly 'disappeared'.

These accounts are a reality. It is very unlikely that hundreds or thousands of women would collectively use the same 'bizarre' identical excuse if they themselves aborted a child and did not wish others to think that they did so, especially when many of these women were the ONLY one's who knew of the pregnancy.

Also, in relation to the apparent 'tug-of-war' between the 'Grey's' and the 'Nordics'/Tau Cetians, etc., over individuals, in an 'Intelligence Report' released by 'Leading Edge Research' (Formerly Nevada Aerial Research). This report stated:

One contactee that has been contacted by the blond/Nordic race was captured and examined (by the Greys) after it was discovered by them that the blue beam used to paralyze people failed to have an effect on him. The implant device that the Nordics put in evidently neutralized the paralysis beam. It was said that the Greys came in a football-shaped craft."

This is one more confirmation, among others, that actual conflict if not warfare exists between various segments of the 'Nordic' Federation and 'Gray' Empire.

Now back to the 'center of the vortex' whereas both Gray and Nordic activity is concerned, that is, the Mojave Desert. In his book, **The UFO Abductors** (1988., Berkley Books., N.Y.), pp 5-6, Rod Steiger describes sighted EBE's in general--

In the greatest number of alien encounters, the UFOnauts were described as standing about five feet tall and dressed in one-piece, tight-fitting jumpsuits. Their skin was gray, or grayish-green, and hairless. Their faces were dominated by large eyes, Very often with snakelike, slit pupils.

They had no discernible lips, just straight lines for mouths. They seldom were described as having noses, just little snubs if at all; but usually the witnesses saw only nostrils nearly flush against the smooth face. Sometimes a percipient mentioned pointed ears but on many occasions commented on the absence of noticeable ears on the large, round head. And, repeatedly, witnesses described an insignia of a flying serpent on a shoulder patch, a badge, a medallion or a helmet.

Lot's of ordinary citizens in the Lancaster area...are having close encounters. . ." Greys participated in animal and human mutilations in order to use the animal and Human secretions as a 'liquid protein' food source. And if we are to believe some of the more fantastic accounts of crash-retrievals, such mutilated animal and human organs have been discovered within or among the debris of crashed Grey

92

craft. The 'Reptile' hierarchy seem to operate in an exactly opposite manner as the Judeo-Christian ethic, and instead of operating on faith, love and service the Reptoid or sauroid hierarchy is said to operate on fear, hatred and competition.

Since both Greys and lizard-like Taurians operate on the basis of collective consciousness and are naturally operating according to a hive or racial consensus with many sources, and since they have a similar agenda which seems to be imperial-conquest motivated, they inevetably work together in what Michael Lindemann calls a 'wedding of convenience'. Likewise, mainstream media built upon the Universalist Globalist dogma of Galactic Treaty Law [the *El-Anu* and *Greada Treaties*] also operate in concert with Deep State and Saurian objectives, unwittingly or otherwise.

From one perspective, one should NOT see natural 'iguanas' as being comparable to Greys; for what the green-blooded Greys lack in the way of demonic hatred or contempt for [mesmerized & unaware] humankind, they seem to make up in their profound 'indifference' to human social values, in violation of the Prime Directive we all know and love from the Startrek Series downloaded and articulated by Roddenberry in the 60s.

What was never conveyed to the American people was that "the Prime Directive" is Galactic Law, and predatory Races do not in fact have any legal right to cull, kill and consume Humans merely because humans are weaker or less organized than they are. Over and over again abductees describe the Greys as emotionless and methodical, and seemingly show no sympathy or pity whatsoever toward human suffering or death, but merely look upon it with

93

scientific 'curiosity'. But what never comes up that ought to come up is that Galactic law **forbids** what Greys are doing—**which is Piracy**--on this world in violation of that Prime Directive.

From that perspective, indifference to human life may be no less evil than raging contempt for human life. Either and both are motivating factors behind all kinds of unlawful crimes and atrocities. It is history that highly intelligent predatory 'Races' do exist, whether or not they might have 'mutated' from that pictured in the 3rd chapter of Genesis. If we are to believe that thousands of witnesses who report UFO encounters, then one can reasonably ask the question: *"Where are they originating from now?"* If they had their origin on earth as Brad Steiger suggests, then *Where on earth are these infernal creatures now—all these years after all these suppressed reports?*

A better question might be, *"Where IN earth are they?"* Though a serpent race has largely succeeded in evading scrutiny of most humans living on the surface of this world over, there are many indicators which suggest a subterranean connection -- not only to a large percentage of the UFO phenomena, but also to many of the creatures which lie behind the phenomena as well, especially the Reptoid creatures such as those described by Steiger.

Many individuals within deep military organizations have since come forward and implied that the Greys used these interactions to establish foot-in-the-door treaties with the Military which were never meant to be honored, but were used only as platforms to get control, via implantation and so on, of sensitive government-military personnel. The

Greys are said to have used deception profusely to get their way.

Some of the reasons why the Agreements continue even after the 'Grand Deception' has been discovered, some suggest, is simply because the Greys have taken over the minds of certain officials in high government positions. This continued 'pact' with the serpent Race may also, in part, be explained by the malevolent influence of the 'Jesuit-Illuminati' or the 'Serpent Cult' in certain policy making groups such as 'MJ-12', the Jason Society, etc.

Salvador Freixedo, author of *'Visionaries, Mystics & Contactees* -- Arcturus Book Service -- "was a Jesuit for 30 years until he began discovering that the Roman-Church not only knew a lot about unexplained phenomena, but that it used phenomena as a basis for exercising its stranglehold on the minds and spirits of 700,000,000 'faithful.'

Pope Leo XIII incidentally stated in *'The Great Encyclical Letters'*, p. 304: "We hold upon this earth The Place of God Almighty" The question is... could the serpent race be getting a little help in its attempts to deceive the masses from human collaborators who are nothing more than 'dragons' in doves' clothing? *(After all, do not the Jesuits themselves -- the gnostic serpent or dragon cult which established the Bavarian Illuminati, the Scottish Rite of Masonry and also helped to establish Hitler's SS -- use as their emblem a white 'dove'? - Branton)*

UNDERGROUND LOGISTICS

Tube shuttles take personnel 50 miles to the other end of the base in the Tahachapi mountains. The underground base has been referred to as an underground city. It is even said that there are disks stored in glasslike enclosures under a vacuum to preserve them.

What may very well be a confirmation of the above appeared in the Dec. 1990 issue of a publication sent out by 'The Borderland Sciences Research Foundation', which had for years been under the direction of Riley H. Crabb. The information was in the form of a letter which we quote here:

I spent the weekend with a 'recent' Edwards AFB workman and his wife -- 'recent' because they are both repeat contactees and have become 'unmanageable' as the AFB management puts it. He was fired for blasting a Spybee with spray paint -- which I find funny and as classic as the graffiti on New York subway cars.

"You did it on purpose," they told him, and they knew of course, because the Spybees are telepathic (in other words, capable of 'tuning in' to Extremely Low Frequency or 'ELF' electro-encephalographic neuro-brain wave patterns--*Branton*) as well as camera equipment. They also carry microphones. We were all laughing as he told us how the little spray-painted gold orb, blinded, went bouncing off walls and posts and was quickly withdrawn from its spy mission. He said Spybees are about the size of a basketball. They fly by antigravity all over any 'Above Top Secret' installation. They dart soundlessly everywhere and hover between workers, sometimes programmed to harass the guys for fun, like bumping them in the rear end.

No person that he and his friends knew about there was allowed to say one word to another while on the job. They would test by trying to write to each other in the floor dust. Within two or three strokes a Spybee would whiz around the corner, lock on to and stop above the writing. His last comment was to write and draw a great big 'screw you'.

His painting work was part of an ongoing excavation beneath Edwards AFB on the high DESERT in California. He and his crew were always blindfolded and strip-searched before transit. They couldn't even have watches. by taking turns counting in the elevator going to and from the work site, they estimated it must be some 9,000 feet down, at least two miles, and the trip took about 15 minutes.

Management accused him of doing it on purpose, and they knew... 'No, no. The Spybee kept bumpin the back of my neck while I was sprayin. After one real hard knock I whirled around with the spray gun still goin.'

A prominent researcher with us that Saturday evening suggested, after careful questioning of the worker, that the elevator itself was anti-gravitic, as there were no cables; so the estimated distance was at best minimum. All present confirmed the government's possession of plasmole tunneling machines which melt a 50 foot hole through solid rock, at a rate of about five miles per hour.

For part of the night we went 'foo chasing', their term for sightseeking UFOs. Tahachapi (is) where H. Hughes and Northrup Corporations and the USAF have just imported Delta Forces and fleets of black helicopters deployed by the government for top security events coverage. There is no doubt something major going on up there... even that night.

The researcher and his team were hoping to see the 30- foot version of the spybees, as there are growing numbers of reports on these. They are designed to fly over your house carrying surveillance beams for thought/ emotion control and behavior modification (Note: Since thoughts and emotions may be to some extent electromagnetic in nature, it may be possible for them to be manipulated by EM rays - *Branton*).

I often see Terra now as in near-final throes of exactly the H.G. Wells scenario where the unwilling and witless 90% of mankind inhabits a play-fantasy world on Earth's surface, while the split-off race of highly technical degenerates (in league with and/or controlled by the serpent race? - *Branton*), the Trogs, prey on them from underground...

In previously years most of these people have been terrified at the prospect of telling their stories, for fear of ridicule. Before the abduction phenomena was widely known, many who spoke out about alien experiences actually ended up in psychiatric institutions, so there was at that time a definite danger of talking too much about their horrifying encounters.

Added to this is the official governmental denial of the phenomena, or even outright attempts to silence those who knew too much for supposed National Security reasons (actually it was/is "Establishment Security" they were interested in). However at this point in time when radio, television and even motion pictures are giving the subject another (this time more respectable and honest) look, many more people are gathering the courage to come forward with reports of abductions by malevolent -- or contacts with benevolent A-liens.

In the hidden depths of the Nevada Military Complex a battle is raging. Few know just how long it has been going on. Apparently it began some years ago when the Nevada Test Site workers discovered vast subterranean cavities deep underground, possibly as a result of the underground nuclear blasts which had artificially excavated huge cavities deep below the surface.

This activity apparently corresponded with the same general time-period when the U.S. Secret Government was making deals with the Greys, establishing secret locations such as S-4 to study alien craft that had crashed, and con-structing environmental enclosures for some of the few A-lien beings who were apprehended alive. Much of this activity took place and is taking place within the extreme high-security areas on and below the Nevada Military Complex.

However, reports now coming out of the Complex sug-gest that far more than just a few of the A-lien Greys, and even their Reptoid overlords, are involved with the activities taking place in Nevada... more activity than even a few A-lien survivors of crashed disks could account for.

Many accounts have spoken of vast caverns below the southern Nevada region which may have been ancient lairs of Reptoid hominoids for decades or centuries. All the accounts point to only one possible conclusion: that the Test Site workers broke into the native habitat of these Reptoid beings, or a system of caverns which the Reptoids had taken control of in the recent or distant past.

Possibly in an effort to prevent a unilateral warfare between the two expanding 'worlds', the secret government decided to establish a treaty with the Saurian Greys (apparently the Greys tried to convince the human governments that they had originated from other-stellar regions -- and that the humans had encountered one of their underground "bases" -- in order to steer the humans clear of the fact that many of them were native to the Terran Subterranea.

This may have been a half-lie, as the Reptoids do reportedly have ancient facilities that they have established and entrenched on other planetary bodies). Aside from establishing treaties with the extraterrestrial "Greys" that are apparently returning to their native planet, a secret treaty was also made with their counterparts in the so-called underground bases.

Most of the workers would not be aware of the alien activity taking place in these extreme lower levels due to the higher security clearances necessary to enter or even KNOW of them. This could explain the confusion which seems to exist, and the comments made by workers, especially within the Nevada Military Complex, that everything is way out of control.

It might also explain the comments made by others in the know who suggested that government is in a panic since they have learned that Sauroid A-liens from other stars have infiltrated and undermined the surface of the earth without us even knowing it, and that this is why they are in such confusion, why they are rushing head-long to develop weapons such as Excalibur to destroy subterranean alien strongholds, and so on.

In the movie '*They Live*', which depicted an infiltration of human society utilizing underground 'bases' beneath major cities, one of the human resistance' members asks: "*How long have they been here?*" Later he comes to realize... **"Maybe they've always been here!"**

Perhaps the reason behind the supposed alien infestation and undermining of the underground systems below the surface of the earth could be explained by the possibility that they have ALWAYS been here, or have been for some time. *Do not accounts of Reptoid hominoids date back to prehistoric times when the dinosaurs walked the surface of the earth?* Keep this possibility in mind when trying to fit the following revelations into your framework of reality.

Is it possible that a subterranean race, working closely with others of their kind which long ago left the earth for extra-terrestrial realms, is staging (via subversion, implantation, disinformation, coversion, and infiltration) **a takeover of human society from above and below?**

One group that is allegedly tied-in with the inner workings of the government-alien interactions and/or conflicts is the Delta Force. The Delta's, some claim, have secretly been recruited by the secret government in order to perform certain functions in relation to joint-interaction projects involving deep-level government organizations and the 'A-liens' (Saurian Greys, etc.).

101

At the beginning of these interactions, Government was optimistic about their new-found alliance with an apparently benevolent race of non-human beings. When Government finally discovered the true nature of the Greys and the fact they are using treaties merely as a means to further their internal plans of bringing the human race under their control, then according to various sources 'all hell broke loose!'

Government-CIA in their zeal to establish contact with what they hoped were technological "saviors from the stars" had bargained away much of what they had, including much of the sovereignty of the United States and the World. When the Horrible Truth was discovered, it was too late, the A-liens had already established too much control and their physical and occult conquests were increasing every day. And the Delta's were caught right in the middle.

The Delta Groups (or *National Recon Group*), wear the 'Trilateral' insignia, a black triangle on a red background. 'Delta' is also the fourth letter in the Greek alphabet, which has the form of a triangle. The symbol appears prominently in certain Masonic lodges, and is said to have had it's origin with the A-liens (or Serpent Race).

Delta Forces were the major group who were, according to some sources, involved in the 1979 attempted rescue of several scientists being held captive within the deepest levels of the Dulce complex below northwestern New Mexico. These workers had stumbled across the Horrible Truth; and according to reports, more than 66 Human scientists, military, many of them Delta Force, were slaughtered by the nonhuman inhabitants and controllers of these lower levels.

102

Others allege that Air Force Blue Berets were also involved in this conflict, which was later to become known as the 'Dulce Wars'. Exactly what part the Air Force Blue Berets played, however, is uncertain.

John Lear on hearing this account, became interested in the military-industrial branches of the USGovernment and Alien forces. Lear emphatically states that the A-liens are here and that many of them bode us ill.

It started after World War II, he begins. We [the Allied forces] recovered some Alien technology from Germany -- not all that they had; some of it disappeared. It appears that some time in the late '30s, Germany recovered a saucer. What happened to it we don't know. But what we did get was some kind of ray gun...

During the period 1979 to 1983 it became increasingly obvious to MJ-12 that things were not going as planned. it became known that many more people [in the thousands] were being abducted than were listed on the official abduction lists. in addition, it became known that some, not all, but some of the nation's missing children had been used for secretions and other parts required by the A-liens.

In 1979 there was an altercation of sorts at the Dulce Laboratory. a special armed forces unit was called in to try and free a number of our people trapped in the facility, who had become aware of what was really going on. according to one source 66 of the soldiers were killed and our people were not freed.

By 1984, MJ-12 must have been in stark terror at the mistake they had made in dealing with the EBE's. They had

103

subtly promoted 'Close Encounters of the Third Kind' and 'E.T.' to get the public used to 'odd-looking' A-liens that were compassionate, benevolent and very much our 'space brothers'. MJ-12 'sold' the EBE's to the public, and were now faced with the fact that quite the opposite was true. In addition, a plan was formulated in 1968 to make the public aware of the existence of A-liens on earth over the next 20 years to be culminated with several documentaries to be released during 1985-1987 period of time. These documentaries would explain the history and intentions of the EBE's. The discovery of the 'Grand Deception' put the entire plans, hopes and dreams of MJ-12 into utter confusion and panic.

Meeting at the 'Country Club', a remote lodge with private golf course, comfortable sleeping and working quarters, and its own private airstrip built by and exclusively for the members of MJ-12, it was a factional fight of what to do now. part of mj-12 wanted to confess the whole scheme and shambles it had become, to the public, beg their forgiveness and ask for their support. The other part [the majority] of MJ-12 argued that there was no way they could do that, that the situation was untenable and there was no use in exciting the public with the horrible truth, and that the best plan was to continue the development of a weapon that could be used against the EBE's under the guise of 'SDI', the Strategic Defense Initiative--which had nothing whatsoever to do with a defense for inbound Russian nuclear missiles.

As these words [were] being written, Dr. Edward Teller, 'father' of the H-Bomb [was] personally in the test tunnels of the Nevada Test Site, driving his workers and

104

associates in the words of one, 'like a man possessed'. And well he should, for Dr. Teller is a member of MJ-12 along with Dr. Kissinger, Admiral Bobby Inman, and possibly Admiral Poindexter, to name a few of the current members of MJ-12.

But Science is a learning process, right?. One very interesting account, which seems to indicate that hi-tech human societies on and within the earth did in fact colonize other planetary bodies thousands of years ago, appeared in **Search Magazine** in an article entitled "Brace Yourselves" written by an ex-NASA employee who identified himself only as 'The Doc," in the Winter, 1988-89 issue, he spoke of two very remarkable things that he'd heard while working at NASA during the 80s.

1) One of them included the discovery that the sun's surface may not be a region of continuous thermonuclear activity as has commonly been believed. Instead, scientists had found that it appeared to be in essence a tremendous electromagnetic dynamo or sphere which in turn generates the electromagnetic fields of the planets. In other words it seemed to be more of a gigantic electrical 'light' or 'sphere' than a gigantic thermonuclear reactor, although nuclear reactions might play a part, but not nearly to the extent that many believe.

Secondly, 2) from other NASA employees came a report that the U.S. Navy has for several year been making regular reconnaissance-observation trips to monitor alien 'bubble-cities' on the ocean floor from ages and aeons past.

Before the Grand Deception was discovered and according to a meticulous plan for metered release of information to the public, several documentaries and video tapes were made. William Moore, a Burbank, California, based UFO researcher who wrote, **The Roswell Incident**--a book published in 1980 that detailed the crash, recovery and subsequent cover-up of a UFO with four Alien bodies--has a video tape of two newsmen interviewing a military officer associated with MJ-12.

This military officer answers questions relating to the history of MJ-12 and the cover-up, the recovery of a number of flying saucers and the existence of a live Alien [one of three living A-liens captured and designated, or named, EBE-1, EBE-2, and EBE-3, being held in a facility designated as YY-II at Los Alamos, New Mexico. The only other facility of this type, which is electro-magnetically secure, is at Edwards Air Force Base in Mojave, California.

The officer named as previously mentioned a few others: Harold Brown, Richard Helms, Gen. Vernon Walters, JPL's Dr. Allen and Dr. Theodore van Karman, to name a few of the current and past members of MJ-12. The officer also related the fact that the EBE's claim to have created Christ. The EBE's have a type of recording device that has recorded all of Earth's history and can display it in the form of a hologram.

This hologram can be shown; but because of the way holograms work, it does not come out very clear on movie film or video tape. The crucifixion of Christ on the Mount of Olives (this actually took place on the hill Calvary, not the Mt. of Olives - *Branton*) has allegedly been put on film to show the public. The EBE's claim to have created Christ, which in view of the grand deception could be an effort to disrupt traditional values for undetermined reasons.

UFO Report from Dulce, New Mexico -- FILE: UFO749 – 1988.--SUMMARY: -- Report of UFO sighting over Mt. Archuleta, NM on October 23, 1988 by John F. Gille et. al. LOCATION AND TIME" -- Southern slopes of Mt. Archuleta, 5 miles NW of Dulce, NM. -- Location of the phenomenon: South to North trajectory for about two miles stopping very close to Mt. Archuleta summit. Estimated closest observers distance: 480 yards. -- Distance from observers to spot where the UFO stopped: 510 yards. -- Time: 7:51 pm Mountain time. -- Duration: est. 5-6 seconds

WITNESSES: -- Eliane Allegre, RN -- Gabe Valdez -- Edmund, friend of Valdez -- "Jack" [pseudonym], PhD -- Manuel, local kid -- Greg, son of Valdez -- Jeff, another son of Valdez -- John Gille, PhD

(Note: "Jack" would probably be Jason Bishop, which is itself a pseudonym used by a researcher and a friend of mine who uses this pseudonym because of his deep-level research into some very dangerous areas of investigation. That is, IF one considers the revelations such as those contained within this volume to be 'dangerous' information under certain circumstances. - *Branton*)

CIRCUMSTANCES OF SIGHTING: I [John Gille] was interested in the Dulce area because of rumors related to a jointly [CIA-Alien] occupied underground facility under Mt. Archuleta, and to numerous UFO sightings, as reported by local residents. A night of observation in the mountains had been planned under the leadership of Valdez. Since about 7:30pm, we had been playing OUIJA at the instigation of Valdez.

107

Just as we were processing the last person, one of Valdez's sons shouted: "Look! Here it comes!" [NOTE: I {Gille} DO NOT make the statement that there was a causal correlation between what we had just been doing and what we saw next.

I merely report two consecutive events which may or may not have been correlated.]

THE PHENOMENON: The object came from the south at great speed on a flat, straight, rectilinear, horizontal trajectory resulting in a perfectly straight luminous yellowish line. It was definitely not a plane or a shooting star. There was no sound coming from the object. The object stopped dead in its tracks near the top of the mountain. At the same time, it became extremely luminous, lighting at least half the sky. There was a display of various colors: yellow, pink, green, and a shower of sparks. Then the object folded on itself and disappeared. The trajectory was about 2000 ft. above the lowest point under the estimated path of the object, which is the Navajo River, elevation 6600 ft. END

Former Naval Petty Officer and Intell worker, William Cooper, on January 10, 1989, posted the following statement on a computer network devoted to the investigation of paranormal events: it was extracted from a rather long treatise/ transcript/ conversation between an individual and another who was assigned to Delta Security:

01: Delta security has a lot to do with inter-service projects.

02: The Trilateral insignia (A-lien) is valid and has been used to mark equipment.

03: 'The whole thing is grim and won't get any better.'

04: The Trilateral insignia has been seen on a disk at Edwards AFB, CA and Area 51 in NV.

05: There is a hanger at Edwards referred to as the Delta Hanger.

06: The Delta Hanger is on the North Base at Edwards.

07: You need a special badge to get near it. It is a red badge with a black triangle on the face of it and personal information on the back.

08: Disk in hanger at Edwards described as having insignia on the underside and on the top. It was about 50' in diameter, appearing like tarnished silver, about 15 to 18 feet thick. There were what looked like windows around the raised portion that were mostly described as rectangular. There was a groove around the disk about 4 feet from the edge all the way around. There was an area on the bottom that looked like vents or louvers.

09: When people assigned to Delta would break down and cry for no apparent reason, you would never see them again.

10: Apparently, the NRO (National Recon Organization) recruits for DELTA out of Fort Carson, Colorado.

11: Just about everyone assigned to DELTA are orphans, they have no relatives, etc.

12: There are bounty hunters connected with Dreamland who earn prize money by targeting dissent.

13: If you work at Dreamland and go on leave or are not back on time they send 'bounty hunters' after you. That's where the 'visitors' live...there is an underground facility...

14: Area 51 is at Groom Lake in Nevada. The disks are flown there.

15: One of the craft looked like an upside-down diamond.

16: There is a radiation hazard apparent when some of the craft fly; instruments onboard incite concern.

17: No one stays at Dreamland for more than a few months.

18: 'Everything is way out of control..'" (no longer under 'human' control? - *Branton*)

PROJECTS: Blue Beam, Sign, Grudge, Aquarius, Signa, Pluto, Snowbird, Luna, Gabriel, Excalibur (1988)... (Note: These are some of the 'secret projects' allegedly relating to the U.S. Government's interaction with the UFO phenomena. Further details on these projects are available from Leading Edge Research., P.O. Box 481-MU58., Yelm, WA 98597.

Although L.E.R. carries much documentable information from very reliable sources, the reader should be warned that they also carry some 'occult channeled' information which may be of an extremely dubious nature, information that cannot be physically substantiated. But the 'documentation' it does carry is extensive and very well compiled - *Branton*.

Since the late 1960's, bizarre animal (especially cattle) mutilations have been on the increase. Numerous accounts claim that these mutilations were performed with laser-fine surgical precision, with cuts so precise (down to the separation of the molecules themselves) that they could not have been accomplished by the conventionally known technology of the time. Eyes, colons, reproductive organs, etc., are very often reported as having been removed in such a manner as if part of a rehearsed process being carried out in widely scattered locations.

The blood is almost always described as having been drained with no resulting vascular collapse (also impossible with the conventional technology of our society at the time). In most cases no tracks or markings in the ground have been discovered, which is another mystery that investigators for a large part have been unable to explain; but in the few cases where markings have been seen, the investigators consistently report the existence of strange 'tripod' or 'crop-circle' marks in the ground, nothing else.

Another strange phenomena surrounding these mutilations is the fact that predatory birds and other animals which have fed off the carcasses of the mutilated animals have often been found lying dead nearby. It is even reported that in some cases maggots have refuse to touch such carcasses. Again, the reason is unknown. *Just who or what is mutilating these animals?* The "Mutilation" phenomena was at its height from the mid-1970's to the late 1980's. In the mid-1990's the mutilations seem to have had a major resurgence, especially throughout the Rocky Mountain states. In the Vol.5, No.4, 1990 issue of "UFO" Magazine (pp.16-17), Linda Moulton Howe, in her article, "***The harvest continues: animal mutilation update***" made some very remarkable observations concerning the mutilators themselves. She wrote:

> In 1989, there were so many cattle mutilations in southern Idaho that Bear Lake County Sheriff Brent Bunn told me: 'We haven't seen anything like this since the 1970's. Sheriff Bunn sent me 16 neatly-typed Investigation Reports about cattle mutilations that had taken place in his county between May and December. Over half occurred in a remote valley called Nounan. Only eighty people lived there. Ranching is their main income source, and cattle are precious. Disease and predators are old and well-understood enemies. What descended on Nounan, Idaho in the summer and fall of 1989 was not understood -- and it scared people.
>
> 'Bloodless cuts -- that's what bothers people,' officer Greg Athay wrote in his mutilation report, There were no visible signs of the cause of death. It appeared that only the soft tissues (nose, lips and tongue) were gone off the head and four nipples off the bag. Again there was no blood on the hair and ground.'

Howe described another incident which took place in this region during the same time-period. This series of mutilations involved mostly cattle, over half of which were young calves:

> One mutilated calf, found December 24 (1989), north of Downey, Idaho, was found lying on its back with the naval, rectum and genitals neatly cut out of the steer's white belly. No blood was found anywhere. The steer was taken for an autopsy to Dr. Chris Oats, D.V.M., at the Hawthorne Animal Hospital. Dr. Oats checked all the vital organs and was unable

to determine the cause of death. During the autopsy, a sharp cut was found in the right chest area, and Dr. Oats also discovered that a main artery had been severed under the chest wound. She was surprised that 'the steer had lost a large amount of blood, but (she) could not understand where it went to. There was no blood on the steer or on the ground. Dr. Oats also determined that the steer had not been dragged by the neck or tied up around the feet.

Abductions resuming in the late 80's **meant something was going on** in the present tense among ET's in the Four Corner Area. In the mid-1980's a Canadian woman by the name of Joan Howard wrote a privately published book, entitled, *The Space--or Something-- Connection*. We refer to it here because it dealt with some experiences which she, or rather her husband, had shortly after she came to America from Britain involving incidents that took place while he was doing some field work for a certain company, travweling through some relatively unpopulated terrain in West Virginia, particularly in the regions between Newville in Braxton county, and Helvetia in Randolph county, or rather the general region in and around the northern part of Webster county.

During their travels through the forests and wilderness, and the rolling hills-mountains of West Virginia, he encountered caverns which contained strange hieroglyphic-like writing on it's walls, and others claimed that they heard what sounded like faint voices and also machine-like sounds moving underground. One of the employees claimed that, while exploring the labyrinthine depths of a particular cavern in the area, he had suddenly come face to face with a woman. She was attractive yet completely devoid of hair (such as

113

someone who might have been subjected to radiation poisoning?). The woman, who spoke a language completely foreign to the man, tried for some time to communicate. After they found that they were not getting anywhere, they departed and went their separate ways.

Stan Deyo was one of many Air Force cadets during the 1960's who dreamed of serving his country as an Air Force pilot. That was until Deyo learned that something strange was going on in the Air Force Academy where he was stationed. Deyo had enlisted into the United States Air Force and was sent for special training to the highly prestigious Air Force Academy located in Colorado Springs, Colorado.

We were the elite from all over America, especially selected for a secret purpose we knew nothing about,' he told PEOPLE MAGAZINE, an Australia weekly news magazine not to be confused with the celebrity profile magazine of the same name published in the U.S. 'They got control of our minds when we were asleep and fed us the most advanced physics for months on end. Then some of us began to realize something was happening to our minds and we rebelled.

After two years, they failed the entire class -- 180 of us. We knew too much. I'm speaking out now because I believe the world should know what they are up to, as well as for my own protection.' As Deyo explains it, the Sixties were a turbulent period even as far as the U.S. government was concerned. The CIA in conjunction with military-industrial 'big business' was acting in collusion.

Deyo alleges, on findings that center around the development of a type of disk or saucer-shaped, antigravity

114

machine that originated out of A-lien technology. Accordingly, the U.S. is worried that sooner or later they will run out of conventional fuel sources and that the 'elite' and powerful will need a revolutionary technology in order to survive (and no doubt maintain their control over the populations of the earth--*Branton*).

CIA-DARPA contacted General Electric, Sperry Rand and Bell Aircraft to spearhead a drive to develop new technology which can whirl a disc-like craft through interplanetary space at thousands of miles a second using the minds of the craft's crew members to navigate the Earth-made UFOs. This is where Deyo's training was supposedly to come in handy. Because of his intelligence level, he was to be made one of the ship's pilots as soon as his mental capabilities had been 'stretched' through hypnosis and an advanced form of electronic mind control.

SECTION 7: THE 1990s

In the Spring, 1991 issue of "UFO JOURNAL OF FACTS" (Box 17206., Tucson, AZ 85710), researcher Forest Crawford gives a report by a former deep-level government employee who Crawford refers to only as 'Oscar' describing inner-earth military transport. Oscar is a simple country person from rural Missouri where he lives with his wife, three children, and a menagerie of stray animals.

QUOTE : "We proceeded down six flights of stairs below the Comtrapac submarine base in San Diego to 'shoot-the-tubes.' After placing a few pieces of jewelry in a container I climbed into the cylinder to travel the tunnels to an unknown assignment. I wondered what was so important to upgrade our pay from E-3 to E-6 before we left and besides that, we could not even finish breakfast.

"'As I am told of our departure, a familiar uneasy feeling comes over me. When you push down on the accelerator in your car, one can feel the tug of inertia sinking you into the seat. When you travel the tubes there is no feeling of motion but you know when the door opens you will be in another place hundreds, even thousands of miles away. For some comfort I checked to see if the watch hidden in my pocket was still there. I quickly looked to see if it is still running. It seems to be working normally, so why no jewelry? Because of electrical charge buildup perhaps?

"The soft clang of the door opening made me tense again. I did not even feel us stop! Peeking at the watch I noted only 30 minutes had passed. We must be in California, Nevada or Arizona, I thought."

Forest Crawford continues:

He (Oscar, based on what the EBE 'Hank' communicated to him) claims that they are also kidnapping children. The Tau Cetians have been preyed upon by these A-liens before and they are working with other races and communities that were also victims. One such race that oscar claims was run off their home planet by the bug people was what we now call the Nordics or Pleiadians. He claims, because of his ongoing contacts, he was made aware of the Billy Meier case in Switzerland and swears that is a real contact...

As Oscar told the story that began this article it became obvious that, because of his military background, the name given was for his protection. The account unfolded further to reveal horrible injustices to a detained E.T. and to Oscar himself. At the direction of Drake the team conducted medical experiments such as spinal taps, marrow sampling, taking organ specimens and other exploratory surgery on the E.T. WITHOUT anesthesia.

Oscar had spent many hours over three months communicating with and growing close to the alien. One day he stepped between Drake and his ET-detainee with his .45 cal. pistol drawn and demanded an end to the torture. Drake withdrew but the next morning Oscar had new orders to depart immediately for Saint Albans Hospital in Radford, Va., where he was incarcerated for debriefing.

He remained isolated for several months until the efforts of Lt.(?) Charles Turner, Oscar's Commanding Officer, got him to move to a psychiatric ward. His family, who had now been out of touch with him for almost three months,

117

was told that Oscar had suffered a head injury during a submarine accident. After spending time under psychiatric care, which would damage his military record, he was oddly enough given an honorable discharge.

After having returned to civilian life he and his father embarked on a hiking trip to North Dakota. They purposely entered the restricted area surrounding the base where Oscar had been stationed. Perimeter patrol picked them up for removal from the area. While in their company Oscar asked how Hank was doing. One of the guards confided that the alien had died several months earlier."

The following is a quote from Matt Spetalnick's article, "Is Anybody Out There? NASA looks for Real ET's", in *Reuters Magazine,* Oct. 5, 1992:

At least 70 times scientists have picked up radio waves that bore the marks of communication by beings from other worlds, but they were never verified, [Frank] Drake said. And researcher John Spencer, in a reference to Dr. Otto Strove, tells how this astrophysicist assisted Frank Drake in establishing Project OZMA, and it's very mysterious conclusion: "...the project began its search by focusing on the star Tau Ceti. According to claims made at the time, As soon as the project got underway strong intelligent signals were picked up, leaving all the scientists stunned. Abruptly, Dr. Strove then declared Project OZMA had been shut down, and commented that there was no sensible purpose for listening to messages from another world.

The Battle for Dulce

But there is this government that has known about the alien presence for a long time, a government that has been playing an end game. A government that has an agenda of concealment and control, that is operated by terror. In Lancaster, that agenda of concealment and control is what I call the 'Lancaster Syndrome'. It produces strange distortions in many peoples lives... First let me tell you about a man who sits today in Pierce County jail outside of Tacoma, Washington. This man's name is Michael Riconosciuto...

Lindemann states that Riconosciuto formerly worked for a corporation called Wackenhut which provides special security protection for high-security areas such as the Nevada Test Site. Michael R. claims that the real reason he was sent to jail was because he swore out an affidavit against the Dept. of Justice. In that affidavit he explained that the U.S. Dept of Justice had swindled the private company Inslaw out of a proprietary software called PROMIS. This software was a database designed to track special groups of people according to various characteristics. It was a very powerful, very capable database. Inslaw developed this in the early 1980's and took it to the Dept. of Justice thinking it would be a good law enforcement software. The software would be most useful in helping He postponed at that time a decision on punitive damages which could run as high as $25,000,000. And as it happens, all of that is all in appeal. The justice dept. was not at all pleased with that ruling. It does state that justice is in a sorry state in America. If you didn't know that already, I hope this helps you to understand.

Michael was responsible for doing the modifications on the PROMIS software before selling that software to the Canadian government after it was 'stolen' from INSLAW, and

119

so he had an inside track on this information, Lindemann stated.

He explained that the Dept. of Justice, among other things, prevailed on him in Feb. of this year (1991) NOT to offer his information in the ongoing lawsuit. One Dept. of Justice official by the name of Peter Videnicks stated that IF he would cooperate with this request they could promise him certain benefits..." (including an assurance of a favorable outcome in a prolonged custody battle between Michael R. and his ex-wife).

According to Michael R., the Dept., of Justice also outlined specific punishments that I could expect to receive if I did cooperate with the House Judiciary Committee!

Now this is just an indicator, Lindemann states, that the Dept. of Justice definitely has it's own idea of the meaning of justice.

Michael Riconosciuto went ahead and swore out an affidavit against the Justice Dept. alleging grand larceny against the Inslaw Corp. Lindemann stated that none of the threatened punishments ever came about as they found an easier way to frame him--

. . . that is, they busted (framed) him for drugs, and now he sits facing a possible life sentence in the Pierce Co. Jail. But because of that he's very, very scared because he knows now that these guys will take-him-out whenever they damn well feel like it. And so he's talking, he's talking in every way he can. . . .

120

In particular we wanted to ask Michael R. something about some of the things going on at the underground bases. I'd like to read you just a little bit of what Michael Riconosciuto told us recently about that. I asked him, *What did he know about the underground bases in the Lancaster area?*

He said, 'Well, there's extensive stuff in... I call it the 'Edwards position', and then at Nellis over in Nevada, and at the Nevada Test Site.' Then he went on to say, Last summer I had a group of guys bagging a whole bunch of files and records, and some equipment out of Wackenhut and they had a helicopter loaded to the nuts and they got shot down before they could get out of there.

I don't know how many of you noticed, Lindemann continues, but there was an article in the **Los Angeles Times**, the 24th of July of this year–"Fatal Copter Crash at the Nuclear Test Site Probed." Five people were killed when this helicopter went down, and the FAA and the DOE and the National Transportation and safety board all converged on the Nuclear Test Site to figure out what brought this copter down. But you may be assured they will never tell you because it was shot down by Wackenhut, and it contained two pilots and three Wackenhut personnel according to the article.

I said, 'I heard about that. Are you saying that that was a group of, let's say, renegades from the inside who were trying to bolt for the blue and Wackenhut shot them down? Is that your allegation? And he said,

Yep! He said, "I told a handful of people that we were hoping to get a big stash of stuff out of there.

121

I said, Were they trying to get out of Nellis?

He said, No, not Nellis, off the Nuclear Test Site.

And the information they were trying to get out, what did it pertain to?

And he said, Guess! I don't even want to talk about it. The worst!

And I said, The very worst, Hugh?

And he said, 'yep'.

Now I don't know of the 'very worst,' do you? The very worst #1) Really nasty, scary alien stuff. The very worst #2) Really nasty, scary bio-tech . . . bio-engineering stuff. There's all kinds of genetic engineering, some of which has to do with the creation of biological warfare agents, some of which has to do with the creation of strange bacteria, and perhaps new strains of chimpanzees and (perhaps) people. There are very, very weird experiments going on, and I thought, 'O.K., fine, maybe one or the other of those things.

But our conversation continued and it leaned in one direction, so let's just see what he had to say next.

I said, One of your associates seemed to indicate that there was technology operating that would have the appearance of flying saucers, but be absolutely terrestrial. Can you comment on that?

And he said, Sure, we had some propulsion devices that were, let's say, rather astounding.

I said, Is this stuff operational? And he said Oh, yes, it's operational.

I said, O.K., so there are vehicles. Would you say that they belonged in the arsenal, or are they part of a sort of gee-whiz lunatic fringe of science?

And he said, Oh no, they're part of the arsenal. It's not lunatic fringe stuff, it's all well-funded, it's all very real. I've worked on portions of it, I've worked on teams that have worked on this stuff, and I've seen with my own eyes. The only thing that I have been shielded from, is any REAL (alien) contact. That I've never been brought directly in contact with, in fact, that part has been minimized to me.

And I said to him, In the way you've said that, I get the impression that you assume that there are extra-terrestrials (i.e. 'A-liens') around.

And he said, I have no direct knowledge of that, O.K.? That's all. There's alot of strange technology, there's alot of extra-heavy security, O.K.? Anybody who breeches a certain point of security is instantly dead or disappears.

I said, Are you saying that given all the other indis-cretions you've shown over the years, that this one would be worst?

And he said, Yes, I would say so.

I said, really?

He said. 'Yes, Yes! It's like those people who were leaving the Nuclear Test Site, they were summarily blown out of the sky.

Now, Michael knew (he was talking on a prison tele-phone - his phone was tapped) indeed, that people who talk too loud, in too much detail about the actual A-lien situation are liable to run into severe problems. Being that he's already in prison and a sitting duck, he's obviously very careful with his words. *But we have talked with some other people who have been more forthright about what they have actually seen in the underground bases.*

One of our sources is a construction worker. He came out of Vietnam, he was a very decorated Special Forces soldier. Among other things he got the Congressional Medal of Honor. And because he was special forces in the Vietnamese war, when he came back stateside he was offered all kinds of bizarre jobs in top security. He felt that those would be too restrictive so he went into construction instead. But because of his military record he had an inside track on a security clearance. He wound up doing construction in the underground bases.

Now you see, the underground installations are built just like a building is built. You know, you've got to do electrical conduit, you've got to paint the walls! Whose going to do it? It's not going to be the Secretary of Defense. It's going to be a guy like our guy! It's going to be like this fellow whose got a Congressional Medal of honor and now does special electrical conduiting underground. So he's told us what he saw.

There's a facility called Haystack Butte, it's on the Edwards (AFB) reservation ... Lindemann shows a map of the area encompassing Edwards AFB, the city of Lancaster and Palmdale to the south – where underground facilities are maintained by MacDonnell Douglas, and the Helendale Facility administered by Lockheed. In this same general area is Haystack Butte which is 'jointly' administered, with North

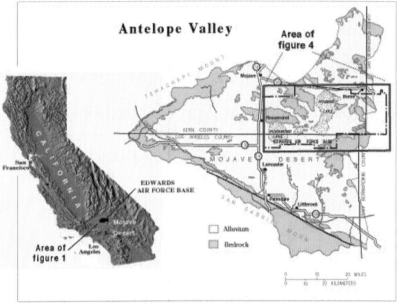

Figure 1—Location of study area.

American Rockwell involved as well.

So what we have here is a situation where you've got our major aerospace companies heavily implicated. I mean this is what is meant by the Military-Industrial Complex. These companies are heavily implicated in super, super secret projects, and at the very top they're all cooperating together in slavery and human trafficking justified by ET-Treaty.

All the bidding wars and every thing that you see are like mid-level smoke and mirrors. But at the very top we're talking about projects that are conducted by all these

125

different people pooling their resources, pooling their information, and indeed pooling their money, which comes in incredible profusion from the Black Budget.

How many of you have seen the book *Blank Check*?... It is not a UFO book . . . so you can understand something about how these projects are funded **without your and my say-so**, *indeed without the say-so of Congress*. Most citizens don't know for example that the National Security Act of 1947 made it illegal to ever say how much money is spent on the CIA; indeed all of our tremendous alphabet soup collection of Intelligence Agencies. Whether your talking about the CIA, or the NRO, or the NSA or the DIA, etc., all of them are in the *same administrative Codes category, classified.*

You cannot say how much these things cost. All you can do if you want to find out is add-up the numbers on the Budget which at this writing is at a deficit of well over $21 trillion (2018) dollars, a large portion of which may have been spent on construction for the underground nation --not assigned to anything that actually means anything to Congress. There are these huge categories that have tens of billions of dollars in them that say nothing but Special Projects. . . And every year the Congress dutifully passes this bloated budget that has some $300,000,000,000 or more with HUGE chunks of cash labelled like that, Special Projects, Unusual Stuff. - Ten billion dollars. O.K., well where does the unusual stuff money go? Well, it DOES go to unusual stuff, that's for sure, and one of the places it goes is...into the underground bases. Indeed TIM said recently since the publication of *Blank Check* . . . more Black Budget money goes into underground bases than any other kind of work.

Now I don't believe that $35 billion, which is the approximate size of the black budget money that you can find by analyzing the budget, I don't think that comes close to the real figure because there is absolutely unequivocal evidence that a great deal of additional money is generated in other ways, such as surreptitious running of guns and drugs. And one wonderful example of that is coming to light with the B.C.C.I. scandal . . . a number of very high-ranking American officials are caught in the undertoe of the BCCI tidal wave.

Indeed the entire end game is very vulnerable and that's why they feel it requires such secrecy. The American people wouldn't stand for this stuff if they had the information, and that's the reason why we have to get the information out and take it seriously because it really is a matter of OUR money and OUR future that's being **mortgaged** here.

A man spoke up who worked in the underground bases, who was doing sheetrock was down on, he thinks, approximately the 30th level underground... These bases are perhaps 30-35 stories deep (ground-scrapers as opposed to a sky-scrapers - *Branton*). As I say they are not just mine shafts, these are huge, giant facilities. . . . many city blocks in circumference, able to house tens of thousands of people.

One of them, the YANO Facility (we're told... by the county fire dept. director, the county fire dept. chief who had to go in there to look at a minor fire infraction) there's a 400-car parking lot on the 1st level of the YANO Facility, but cars never come in and out, those are the cars that they use INSIDE.

O.K., so... a very interesting situation down there. Our guy was doing sheetrock on the 30th floor, maybe the 30th floor underground. He and his crew are working on a wall and right over here is an elevator door. The elevator door opens and, a kind of reflex action you look, and he saw three 'guys'. Two of them, human engineers that he'd seen before. And between them a 'guy' that stood about 8 to 8 1/2 feet tall. Green skin, Reptoid features, extra-long arms, wearing a lab coat, holding a clip-board...

I tend to believe that story because—first of all because we have other stories like it—but more importantly because he walked off that job that very day. And he was getting paid a GREAT deal of money. . . . If your basically a sheetrock kind of guy, if you can do sheetrock in a place like that then you get paid way more than standard sheetrock wages, you can count on it. So, he walked off that job. His buddy on that same crew turned into an alcoholic shortly after.

This is an extremely upsetting thing. You know, it wasn't like this alien jumped out and bit his head off or anything, it was just standing there for a few minutes, the doors closed. He has a feeling that that elevator was malfunctioning, otherwise he never would have seen that except by accident.

In another incident though... at the China Lake Naval Weapons Station, up here at China Lake... near Ridgequest... they were working there on the China Lake Naval Weapons Station and walked by a hanger. . . . They walked by a hanger as they were headed for their trucks to leave for the day. And they had parked their trucks in an unusual place, a place

128

they didn't normally park, because it was an extremely hot day and they wanted to keep the trucks out of the sun.

So the Security had given them permission to park the trucks in a place that wasn't normal. So they walked by a hanger that they didn't normally walk by, and they looked in, just kind of glanced in, and saw inside a couple of Greys working on something. And of course they were, you know, astonished. . . .

And an MP came running over and said: 'Hey, you can't be here! What are you doing here?' And they said: 'Well, Security said we could park our trucks here.'

And (the Security Guard) says: 'Well that's fine, but you get out of here because you'll get yourself killed!' So they left. But one of the young guys on that crew couldn't leave well enough alone.

The guy we've been talking to said, 'Look, I know what you saw, I know what I saw. I know what we saw at Haystack (Butte), it's all for real, I know what's going on, but don't be a stupid jerk. Leave it alone!'

This kid didn't leave it alone, and very shortly thereafter he was booted off the base, and three months later he was dead under mysterious circumstances. Now of course we can't say that he died 'because' of this. There's a disturbing pattern of people dying however when they see things they're not supposed to...

Michael Riconosciuto makes it very clear in his statement to us that if you go past a certain point your dead or disappear, just like that. We've heard that time and time again. Indeed there are a great many people on the 'inside'

129

who are making it clear that they would love to flee, people like these people that apparently were blown out of the sky, the Wackenhut garbage.

These are trained (mercenaries) who have seen things they cannot stand, things that turn their stomach, things that make them want to grab evidence and flee for their lives. And they were blown out of the sky, probably by something equivalent to a stinger missile or something like that. And there are lots of people who want to get out.

Just an example of the way these people talk, one of them said to us, 'I would trade my $100,000.00 a year salary for a job at McDonald's if I could get out alive.

There's a certain despair there, a certain feeling of entrapment. You see there are the people who know what's going on and who have created this agenda and have bought-into it entirely, they are enrolled in it, and they believe that they are indeed the Olympians. They have to employ lots of normal humans like us to do the sheet-rocking, to do the grubwork, and those people are in a very bizarre catch-22, because they are given the promise of a salary that they never believed possible.

You know . . . they're going to paint walls all day and they're going to take down a hundred grand a year, this is unusual. That's the up-side of the deal. The down side of the deal is (you know, and they make it very clear) . . . all these people who get these high security clearances are subjected to incredibly intimidating indoctrination and intimidation processes . . . they really do subject these people to tremendous pressure, tremendous intimidation, indeed they

130

do inflict great violence on people (on whom) they need to. They make examples of people.

In one sense then, there is a growing division taking place between the Constitutionalists of America and the 'Alien' controlled segments within the underground bases. This would also include their human 'pawns' who will apparently do anything, even murder their fellow human beings, in order to continue receiving the technological 'benefits' from their alien masters, to whom they have 'sold' themselves and whose agenda of control and subversion they are serving, whether knowing or unknowingly.

The following is a transcript of parts of a speech presented by Norio F. Hayakawa, director of the Civilian Intelligence Network, at the 11th *Los Angeles Whole Life Expo'* held at The Los Angeles Airport Hilton Convention Center on November 16 and 17, 1991. The transcript from which we will quote is a revised and expanded version of the address written on June of 1992 and is titled -- 'UFO's, the Grand Deception and the Coming New World Order':-- [change in font delineates quote from that Conference.]

AREA 51 is located in the northeastern corner of a vast, desolate stretch of land known as the Nevada Test Site (a large portion of which includes the Nellis Air Force Test Range) but has practically nothing to do with underground nuclear testing. It is located approximately 125 miles north-northwest of Las Vegas and consists of Groom Lake and the Papoose Lake Complexes. The presently expanding eastern portion of the latter complexes is known as the S-4 site.

This entire area is under the strictest control of Airspace R-4808N (with unlimited ceiling), prohibiting any entry therein of air traffic, civilian or military, unless special clearance for such entry is secured well in advance. By land, the area is meticulously patrolled 24-hours a day by several tiers of external security even through it is conveniently covered by the... Jumbled Hills (north of the Papoose Lake area), making it virtually impossible for anyone to see the facilities without first climbing atop the hills of the rugged mountain range which became off-limits to the public since 1985.

The main external perimeter security is now being handled by Wackenhut Special Securities Division, part of the operations of Wackenhut Corporation, a worldwide semi-private security firm based in Coral Gables, Florida which has an exclusive contract with the U.S. Department of Energy and handles not only the perimeter security at the Nevada Test Site but also at many other secret facilities and sensitive installations throughout the U.S., and U.S. interests worldwide, including ground-level perimeters for several large underground facilities in and around Edwards Air Force Base in Southern California.

We must mention that dozens of unmanned, miniature, remote-controlled automatic security vehicles constantly patrol immediate perimeters of the S-4 Site, located around (and presently expanding particularly towards the eastern portion of) Papoose Lake. These automatic, miniature- sized four-wheel vehicles have been produced by Sandia Laboratories of Albuquerque, New Mexico exclusively for the Department of Energy.

The outer northeastern perimeters of this area located in the Tickaboo Valley come under the geographical jurisdiction of Lincoln County and are relegated to the Bureau of Land Management (B.L.M.). Yet it is considered highly unadvisable for anyone to even enter the main country dirt road, known as the Groom Road, which begins its southwestern extension towards Groom Lake from a point midway between mile marker 34 and 33 on Highway 375, and leads to the guard shack located two and a half miles northeast of the Groom Lake complexes.

The first line of exterior security forces (dressed in military- type camouflage uniforms but with no insignia of any kind whatsoever) consists of the GP patrols (the 'Groom Proper' patrols, in Bronco-type four-wheel drive vehicles) who sometimes drive around at night with their lights off on various country dirt roads adjacent to the outer demili- tarized zone, intimidating any civilian vehicle that tries to enter those access roads (off of Highway 375) located on public land. The GP patrols themselves (part of Wackenhut Special Securities Division), however, are strictly ordered to avoid any direct contact with civilians. They are only instructed to radio the Lincoln County Sheriff immediately should anyone be spotted driving on any of those dirt roads. The most common radio frequency used between Security Control and Lincoln County Sheriff's patrols is 138.306 MHZ.

The only congregating area allowed by the local Sheriff for curiosity seekers is an open area near a black mailbox located at the south side of Highway 375 between mile marker 29 and 30. Even then, the Sheriff patrol will routinely stop by during the evening to check on the cars parked at the mailbox area.

133

Moreover, it is our understanding, based on information provided by a highly reliable source connected to a special U.S. Navy SEAL operations center, that the mailbox area is constantly being monitored by high-powered, state-of-the-art, infra-red telescopes set up at a facility known as Security Control high atop Bald Mountain (10 miles west of the area), the highest peak in the Groom Mountain Range.

It was precisely at 4:45 a.m. on the morning of Thursday, April 16, 1992, that an NBC news crew, dispatched to the area to report on the landing of an alleged super spy-plane known as Aurora on Groom Lake, accidentally succeeded in video-taping the first flight (which we have been calling the 'Old Faithful') of [a] mysterious object while standing at the mail-box area and looking due south toward Jumbled Hills.

Their footage, taken with a night-scope vision camera, was broadcast nationally on NBC Nightly News with Tom Brokaw on April 20, 1992. The NBC News reported that it had video-taped a test flight of a new U.S. aerial craft that had definitely defied the laws of physics, and that the news team may thus have taken the first glimpse of the other 'deep black' projects (aside from the Aurora project) being conducted within the confines of the top-secret facility.

Also in regards to the ongoing program, it is to be noted that usually a day or two prior to significant test flights (i.e., only if the test flight is a significant one, by whatever measure known only to the installation) a vehicle-traffic counter is laid on Highway 93, at approximately a mile and a half north of Ash Springs, right before the juncture of Highway 375. The other counter is set up about a half mile or so west upon entering Highway 375. The obvious question is: in such desolate, less-traveled areas of Nevada, why should there be such traffic counters installed on undivided, lonely highways? It is now my belief that the number of cars being registered that head out west on Highway 375 at such times (particularly in clusters such as caravans) is relayed to several of the security posts at AREA 51, including the main observation post high atop the previously mentioned Bald Mountain. However, it is very possible that they may now have more sophisticated devices for registering the number of vehicles going through the area."

In the early 1990's a high-level Intelligence Worker in the U.S. Government who refers to himself only as Commander X for his own protection, 'spilled the beans' on a key secret concerning the interaction and conflict taking place below the Mojave Desert, against the Grey Empire which had entrenched itself in the subterranean levels of the Southwest [which had occurred during the 1980's].

The underground...base outside of Dulce, New Mexico, is perhaps the one MOST FREQUENTLY referred to. It's existence is most widely known, including several UFO abductees who have apparently been taken there for examination and then either managed to escape or were freed just in the nick of time by friendly forces.

According to William Cooper, '...a confrontation broke out between the human scientists and the A-liens at the Dulce underground lab. The A-liens took many of our scientists hostage. Delta Forces were sent in to free them but they were no match for the Alien weapons. Sixty-six people were killed during this action. As a result we withdrew from all joint projects for at least two years...'

(Note: the real name of the source of information described in the following paragraph was withheld and known only as T.C. or Thomas C.. We have now been authorized to reveal the full name of the former Dulce Base worker as being Thomas Edwin Castello, who possessed a Level-7 ultra security clearance within the Dulce facility, and who was in fact a head of Security within the underground installation. There are unconfirmed reports that Thomas Castello, after years in hiding, has finally passed away in Costa Rica. Whether or not his alleged death had anything to do with his intimate knowledge of the underground bases, is not known - *Branton*)

T.C [Costello] had seen tall Reptoid Humanoids at the base. This is interesting to me because in 1979 I came face-to-face with the over 6 foot tall Other Species (Reptoids) which materialized in our home! They took blood from my wife (who is an Rh-negative blood type); & her daughter, who was 1500 miles away.

We all came to know that the 'Visitors' were here to stay. We also learned how the Reptoid Race was returning to Earth & the Greys -- who are mercenaries – were being used to interface (with) & manipulate humans. Their agenda was to keep earth surface mankind confused & unaware of their true nature & potential... also to conceal knowledge of vast & varied civilizations living inside and within the Earth.

The Fantastic Truth was made to seem a fantasy, a legend, a myth, an illusion! But Reptoids have returned to earth to use it as a staging area, in their ancient confrontation with the Elohim (the Creator and the Angelic forces as described in Revelation chapter 12, who are not to be confused with the 'ELs' with whom the Reptoids are ALSO in conflict - *Branton*).

There is a vast network of Tube Shuttle connections under the U.S., which extends into a global system of tunnels & sub-cities . . . Reptoids do not consider themselves A-liens... they claim Terra--3rd from the Sun--was their home before we humans arrived.

As a species, the Reptoid heritage beings (Greys, Reptoids, Winged Draco with two horns, a classic stereotype of the Devil, are highly analytical & technologically oriented. They are seriously into the sciences of automation, computers & bio-engineering genetics! However, their exploits in these areas has led to experimentation with total disregard for empathy or "human rights," as we call them. This is also true of many of the human beings working with them!.

The REAL reasons for the incitation of the Dulce Wars: Level #7 is the worst--row after row of 1,000's of humans and human-mixture remains in cold storage. Here too are embryos of humanoids in various stages of development. Also, many human childrens' remains in storage vats. *Who are (were) these people?*

The sources for these incredibly disturbing allegations aside from Thomas Castello included people who worked in the labs, abductees taken to the base, people who assisted in the construction, intelligence personnel (NSA, CIA, etc.), and UFO-Inner Earth researchers. This information is meant for those who are seriously interested in the Dulce base. For your own protection, be advised to use caution when speaking about this complex.

The following is a quote from Matt Spetalnick's article, "Is Anybody Out There? NASA Looks For Real ET's," in **REUTERS Magazine**, Oct. 5, 1992:

At least 70 times scientists have picked up radio waves bearing the marks of communication of beings from other worlds, but they were never verified, [Frank] Drake said. Through proposed projects such as SETI [*Search For Extraterrestrial Intelligence*] involvings large arrays of Radio Dish receiving mechanisms to tune in to cosmic radio waves, Drake and others hoped to contact outside intelligences.

However, if the incidents related by Forest Crawford earlier in this File are correct, this has already occurred. If our tax dollars are going toward other SETI type experiments, chances are that the public will not and never be officially told of the outcome, if they [once again] receive signals from other nearby stars. Such a disclosure might threaten the psychologicalcontrol which the (secret) government has imposed on the nations.

The secret government does not wish to allow planet earth to become a member of a benevolent Federation of Human Worlds, as the Federation policies would certainly condemn the horrendous human trafficking, guns-, drugs-, and body-parts commerce spread across this Galaxy now by the Secret Space fleet.

Power-games Illuminati have used for centuries actually keep mankind in its stranglehold of slavery according to the *Greada* [and previous *El-Anu*] *Treaties.* Illuminati will only ally themselves with **A-liens encumbered by no earthly "liens" nor Ethics** (such as Reptoid/ Greys and some branches of the Ashtar/Astarte network which collaborates with Illuninati-Nazis and Greys in the past). Those ideologies share a desire to wield absolute god-like empirical control over worlds, our Moon and Sun.

Incidentally, another possible use of radar-dish antennas has been suggested by K.S. of Salt Lake City, Utah, who allegedly talked to a man who was involved in setting up top secret underwater radio dishes for secret government projects. He claimed that many of these dishes were used to communicate with bases on the moon and Mars. *If this is the case could the SETI program be, to some extent, an extension of this?*

A February 21, 1990, expedition was instrumental in the production of a two-hour documentary program entitled 'Saturday Super Special' televised throughout Japan on March 24, 1990, that was viewed by more than 28 million viewers on prime time. The entire program dealt with AREA 51 and also the crew's pursuit of an alleged biogenetics laboratory thought to be located just outside of Dulce, a tiny town in northwestern New Mexico, about 95 miles northwest of Los Alamos.

The U.S. Naval Research Laboratory...seems to have a Parapsychology Research Unit that coordinates its research activities with DARPA (Defense Advanced Research Projects Agency). It is my understanding that some of their activities conducted under the auspices of the Office of Naval Intelligence are being held at locations such as AREA 51.

139

ELF (extremely low frequency) wave-emitting devices, scalar machines, electromagnetic beam weapons and highly-defined hologramic projections are just a few examples of the many new types of mind-control weaponry that the government seems to have developed in the past three decades. Newest researches on special types of hallucinatory and memory- tampering drugs are part of a growing 'arsenal' that the U.S. Naval Intelligence boasts to have developed in its own Parapsychology- Mind Control Unit.

According to recent information provided to me by a highly reliable informant within a special operations group of the Department of the Navy, two of the most widely used devices will be R.H.I.C. (Radio Hypnotic Intra-Cerebral Control) and E.D.O.M. (Electronic Dissolution of Memory). The first of the two, Radio Hypnotic Intra-Cerebral Control, calls for the implantation of a very small, electronic, micro-radio receiver. It acts as a Stimulator which will stimulate a muscle or electronic brain response.

This, in turn, can set off a 'Hypno-programmed' cue in the victim or subject, which would illicit a pre-conditioned behavior. The second one, Electronic Dissolution of Memory, calls for remotely-controlled production within the brain of Acetyl-Choline which blocks transmission of nerve impulses in the brain which results in a sort of Selective Amnesia. According to this source, in the hands of certain units within the intelligence community both of these methods are **already beginning to be used!**

In early 1992 Universal Network aired a made-for-TV version of John Carpenter's movie, **They Live.**, which was based on the premise of an alien race of bulge-eyed creatures that had infiltrated human society disguised as humans and who4 were in the process of subtly taking control of powerful social, media, economic and political positions.

They were assisted by a small group of 'human power elite' who through subliminal 'mind control', hidden frequency transmitters, television propaganda, etc., helped to keep the masses in a constant state of semi-consciousness. Those who had not caught-on to the alien conspiracy went about their business in a slightly catatonic state sufficient to keep them 'blind' or 'asleep' to the point that the A-liens and their subversive activities remained just outside of their conscious perception. It is interesting that Carpenter depicted attempts of the A-liens to annihilate human consciousness as a means to minimize human resistance, by destroying individual creativity and programming human "cattle" to conform to dictates of the alien intruders--all of this without humanity even being aware that they were the mind-slaves of an alien force which they were programmed to believe did not exist.

Also in the movie, secret subliminal messages were broadcast throughout all levels of society via all branches of the media, keeping the sleeping masses in a constant state of tranquilized apathy and subservience while yet the A-liens utilized joint underground bases beneath major cities as more-or-less the back-stage of the alien control scenario.

Incidentally, Disneyworld in Florida contains an underground tunnel network with hidden entrances. The employees of the park use these as a 'back stage' -- dressing rooms, employee indoctrination centers and other facilities necessary to keep up the illusion of 'Disneyworld'. John

141

Carpenter in his movie reveals the idea that the huge underground bases beneath major cities are being used as back stages in order to keep an infinitely more diabolical illusion going, with the help of power-elite who assist in the covert subjugation of the masses for personal gain.

In the movie it is the Judeo-Christian element which first 'wakes up' to what is going on, and who begin the revolutionary 'resistance' movement in order to confront a stranglehold of the A-liens upon human society... *Could this scenario be somewhat prophetical as the book of Matthew (13:24-28) seems to suggest?*

"An amazing article appeared in the *Los Angeles Times* on May 12, 1992, announcing that Caltech scientists have recently discovered and confirmed the presence of 'tiny magnetic particles in the brains of humans, similar to those that have heretofore been found in other animals.' (*L.A. TIMES*, Section A, page 3).

According to the Caltech researchers, it is now an undeniable fact that every human brain contains a tiny natural magnetite particle, even from the time of conception. Could the government, particularly the U.S. Naval Research Laboratory, have known this fact for a long time? The answer definitely seems to be in the affirmative!

(Note: Perhaps the Philadelphia Experiment, described in Charles Berlitz' book of the same name, had an adverse affect on the 'electrochemical' or 'magnetite' particles in the brains of the experimental subjects. Could this explain why so many of them allegedly went insane after the 'tests'? - *Branton*)

It is interesting also to note that as of this writing, many strange, turquoise-colored antenna-towers with triangular configurations on top, are beginning to be constructed along key areas near the freeway systems of many U.S. cities, particularly proliferating the Los Angeles and Orange County areas of California. According to several reports, these antenna-towers are presently being used as relay towers for the increasing networks of cellular telephone systems being operated by such firms as Pacific Bell and Telesis.

Yet the most interesting aspect of the constructions of these strange antenna-towers is that there are increasing reports that Department of Defense is somehow involved in this operation. Frequency waves utilized in the cellular telephone communications are, according to several researchers, strikingly close to the range of frequency waves used in several ELF emission and microwave experiments of the U.S. Naval Research Laboratory as well as D.A.R.P.A., the Defense Advanced Research Projects Agency.

(Note: non-digital cellular telephone conversations can be easily intercepted. This writer has succeeded in listening in on cellular conversations by scanning through the upper frequencies of the UHF band on a normal television set! So then, along with the 'mind control' capabilities, it is evident that cellular phone conversations have also been heavily monitored by Military Intelligence - *Branton*) *Will these towers be utilized throughout the nation?*

A large underground genetics laboratory is thought to be located just outside of Dulce, a tiny town in the midst of the Jicarilla-Apache Indian Reservation located about 95

143

miles northwest of Los Alamos and 100 miles east of sinister-sounding Highway 666, the only stretch of highway in the U.S. with that designation and the only highway that links the four states of Arizona, New Mexico, Colorado and Utah.

Perhaps it may just be a pure coincidence that this highway, befittingly named Highway 666, which originated in southeast Arizona and goes up north, cuts into northwestern New Mexico, right near the Four Corners area -- an area that happens to have one of the most consistently concentrated UFO sighting reports in the country since around 1947... This entire Four Corners area, especially northwestern New Mexico and southwestern Colorado also has had some of the most concentrated reports of unexplained cattle mutilations in the nation during the late seventies and early eighties. Was something covertly taking place in those areas?

Even though we could not locate the alleged underground genetics laboratory in Dulce when the Nippon Television crew and I visited the area in late February of 1990, I had several opportunities to interview scores of local residents there that admitted that nightly appearances of mysterious lights (occasionally accompanied by unmarked black helicopters) -- darting over, into and out of nearby Archuleta Mesa and Archuleta Mountains -- were quite common during the late seventies and early eighties.

Many of them even claim to have spotted, on many occasions, military-type trucks and jeeps as well as government vans passing through Dulce and loitering around nearby mesas. Occasionally even black limousines carrying what appeared to be CIA agent-types were claimed to have been sighted loitering around the foothills of other nearby mesas.

We must bear in mind that the Dulce area is only 95 miles northwest of Los Alamos. Los Alamos National Laboratory is one of the top U.S. research laboratories specializing in the study of the human genome. Also it is a vital center of the government's SDI research and development programs. Just about a hundred miles southeast of Los Alamos is Albuquerque, New Mexico's largest city, and more significantly, a city where Kirtland Air Force Base is located right next to the sensitive Manzano Storage Facility, a top-secret underground military facility. Sandia Corporation, one of the nations top-secret government contractors specializing in top military-industrial projects is also located in Albuquerque.

As far as advanced bio-technology is concerned, I have no doubt that a micro-chip implantation technology is being perfected in which tiny micro-chips could be implanted in our circulatory systems, vital organs and tissues if need be for whatever purpose the future may require. It is my conclusion that a large-scale research has been completed by the government (with possible assistance from 'outside' sources) within the last 20 years or so utilizing tens of thousands of cattle in the Southwest to conduct this covert experiment. Only recently has science proven that cow hemoglobin could be substituted (by utilizing a special purification system) with human blood in situations of unforeseen national emergencies. [end of Hayakawa public-domain transcript.]

According to various sources, Area 51 in Nevada, where the S-4, Groom Lake, or Dreamland complexes are located, is the same area where the Stealth Bomber, SR-71, Star Wars or SDI Technology, and all manner of aerospace hightech had been developed and tested; these include CIA experiments and tests. Other names for the Dreamland complex include: 'The Ranch' or "Skunk Works'. This is where Francis Gary Powers, who flew the ill-fated U-2 spy plane mission which was shot down over Russia (where Powers was held prisoner for some time), was trained.

Referring to the subsurface regions, we quote now from the N.A.R. newsletter, which was titled, *'Is Inner Earth Research Hazardous to Your Health?'*

An observation has recently been made that most of the outstanding inner earth researchers have died of heart attack--

[Note: It is interesting that there have been very few if any UFOlogists, etc., who claim to have taken up a devout Christian lifestyle, who have physically suffered the negative side of UFO research -- including encounters with MIBS, abductions, paralysis, heart attacks or other *fear-oriented forms of victimization.* This suggests that a deep FAITH in the Creator may neutralize the FEAR that the A-liens seem to depend on as their major weapon in their psychic attacks against humankind, making the believers impervious to their otherwise destructive influences - *Branton*).

Surely, this is beyond a simple coincidence. **Gray Barker, Dick Shaver,** and **Joan O'Connel** [*New Atlantean Journal*] are but a few (also, researcher **Charles Marcoux** - *Branton*).

Locally, there are several inner earth researchers who are very notable in their persistence. "Lew Tery, who has recently relocated to Utah, was the foremost local proponent of (the) geomagnetic vortex/ UFO connection theory. Lew was instrumental in the discovery of underground tunnel networks in the Las Vegas area, one of them being between the base of Boulder Dam and Jumbo Peak, where there are two mines whose owners view 200' diameter disks on a frequent basis. At one point, Lew offered to set up an interview with these miners. Alas, Mr. Tery is not to be found.

"A local Henderson resident, who shall remain nameless, has been into inner earth research for years. This person has been hounded and chased due to intimate knowledge of inner earth tunnels in the local area. There is obviously something here that some people wish to protect. Something to hide. Many seem to know what it is, and they speak cautiously about **Reptoid humanoids** and the **Serpent Race**, which are two subjects which seem to be surfacing again. Response to local television and radio programs featuring John Lear have been overwhelming. A recent lecture in Las Vegas drew over 700 people.

"*According to some sources, the Greys are the lower level of a bigger scenario that involves this Reptoid race...*"

The following is a transcript of a letter which was sent by John Lear to researcher TAL LeVesque. The letter, dated October 6, 1990, states:

"Dear TAL... Many thanks for your recent, very interesting letter. I showed it to Bob (i.e. Lazar - *Branton*)

147

and he thinks we are both crazy. He does not believe that Dulce exists. Bob went through extreme brainwashing at S-4 so I can understand his feelings. About the time that he was brainwashed, maybe a little before, he told me that Dulce was mentioned up there once or twice in conversations that he was not part of...but that he overhead. Since that time he has forgotten even that part. Since I know Dulce exists, what Bob thinks does not affect me in the least.

"A source of mine that is a security guard at the test site tells me that currently there are 5 types of A-liens there: The Greys, the Orange, the Reptoids, the ones that look like [the A-liens] in the movie 'V' and the ones that look so ugly that they take your breath away until you get used to looking at them. I now believe that a very large Saucer crashed near Sedona, possibly 2 years ago and is in the process of being retrieved in sections, as it is too big to remove in one piece.

"The recent stories in **Aviation Week,** I believe, are attempts to buy more time, to mislead the public and to confuse the issue   (Note: Lear is here referring to the article in the Oct. 1, 1990, issue of **Aviation Week and Space Technology**, titled "Secret Advanced Vehicles Demonstrate Technologies For Future Military Use". The article referred only to the fairly well-known super-advanced jets being tested in Nevada, giving the impression that these may explain all of the UFO sightings in the area – Branton).

"Again, I appreciate very much your fascinating letter and look forward to more information on Dulce... With much respect and admiration... *John Lear*."

The Symbol for the Dulce Base that is worn on many of the workers there, allegedly consists of an UPSIDE-DOWN triangle or pyramid with an upside-down 'T' superimposed over it. William Hamilton added a few comments in his book *Cosmic Top Secret*, concerning studies of the carcasses of mutilated cattle found near Dulce, New Mexico. These include:

...Schoenfeld Clinical Laboratories in Albuquerque analyzed the samples (of the affected hides of cattle studied by Gomez and Burgess) and found significant deposits of potassium and magnesium. The potassium content was 70 times above normal. . . .

...Level 1 (of the Dulce base) contains the garage for street maintenance. Level 2 contains the garage for trains, shuttles, tunnel-boring equipment (or what former Dulce-base worker Thomas Castello refers to as **"the terron drive"** - *Branton*), and disc maintenance. Greys and reptoid species... have had ancient conflicts with Nordic humans from outer space societies, and may be staging here for future conflict.

Penny Harper, in the January 1990 issue of '*Whole Life Times*', wrote an article in which she referred to the UFOlogist and prominent physicist Paul Bennewitz:

Paul Bennewitz -- whereabouts unknown (Note: A search of a major laser-disc U.S. telephone database in 1993 revealed only one listing for 'Paul Bennewitz' -- at 120 E. Pebble Beach Dr., Tempe, AZ 85282 -- telephone #602-966-

5704. This may or may not be the 'Paul Bennewitz' in question - *Branton*).

Paul was a scientist investigating an abduction case. A woman and her son drove down a road in the southwest, the woman witnessed A-liens mutilating a calf. The A-liens captured both mother and son, taking them into an underground installation. The woman saw many frightening things, apparently much of it similar to what abductees Christa Tilton, Judy Doraty and others had witnessed, yet they -- mother and son -- also saw, according to Penny Harper: ...human body parts floating in a vat of amber liquid.

After a horrifying ordeal, the woman and her son were taken back to their car. Bennewitz was able to determine that there is a secret 'alien' base beneath Dulce, New Mexico. He wrote '**The Dulce Report**' and sent it to the civilian UFO group called APRO (i.e. *Aerial Phenomena Research Organization*). Bennewitz was then committed to the New Mexico State Hospital for the mentally ill where he was given electro-shock 'therapy.' When he was discharged, he publicly stated that he would not have anything to do with UFOs. He is a recluse today, but still alive, last I heard.

On Oct. 16th, 1992, FOX Network's 'SIGHTINGS' document- ary described several abduction experiences involving Greys and larger 'Reptoid' entities. One woman alleged that during one encounter with the Reptoid Greys she saw a 'preying mantis' type of creature working with the Saurian Greys and which seemed to be the leader. It had large black eyes, and this is not the only case where reptil-Saurian 'predators' and Insectoid 'parasites' (as some have referred to them) have been seen working together.

150

Just what are these 'Mantis' like creatures that have been seen working with the Greys-Reptoids? Some have suggested that they are an extreme mutation of the Reptoid race, while others suggest they are interdimensional entities of insectoid configuration.

John Lear has alleged that one of the first crash-retrievals of an unidentified aerial disk involved these 'mantis-like' creatures which were found on board. However he also states that within a short period following the incident ALL of the high government officials who investigated that particular case died under mysterious circumstances.

Such a coincidence may seem sinister if not demoniacal in nature. Like the Reptoids themselves, these Mantis-like creatures have usually been described as being deadly and very deceptive and abusive. It seems as if they operate on an equal basis, and in some cases a superior basis to the so-called Reptoid and Saurioid Gray alien groups and possibly the pterodactoids or so-called 'Mothmen' as well.

Another unconfirmed source claimed to have seen huge Mantis-like individuals in a cavern deep below a drill-shaft south of the Kokoweef mountain area near the Mojave Desert. The account, rather obscure in some details, was related by way of a Mr. Stolz who knew some individuals involved in modern attempts to break into Earl Dorr's legendary 'underground grand canyon' or river of gold beneath Kokoweef peak.

It is uncertain whether the man in question was lowered down the hole or whether he allegedly saw the

151

creatures via camera equipment that was lowered down the drill-shaft.

ORION BASED TECHNOLOGY, MIND CONTROL AND OTHER SECRET PROJECTS -- A SERIES OF CONDUCTED INTERVIEWS, 53 pg, $8.00:

This 53-page report was constructed from over 9 hours of video interviews, personal interviews and individual commentary. It is structured in an open question-answer format in such a way that the identities of the different parties are protected. This was requested by several of the parties in order to permit this piece of work to be done and disseminated. It took approxi- mately 20 hours of work to create the report, which contains information about some of the following topics:

The Philadelphia Experiment or

Project Rainbow,

Phoenix Projects 1-3,

Radiosonde

work of Wilhelm Reich,

Govt weather control agenda,

Montauk Mind Control

time-tunnel projects

Nickola Tesla & Von Neumann

the martyrdom clause,

mind control by individual signature,

ways to produce planetary holograms

Maitreiya effects...

Govt rationale for camps and slavery,

Project Dreamscan,

Project Moonscan, the

Airborne Instrument Labs,

Project Mindwrecker,

Alien group Kondrashkin

the Kamogol II and Giza Groups,

the negative Sirians,

Soviet scalar weaponry,

Orion Group manipulations...

telepathy producing drugs

FAA and zero-time generators,

technical spin-offs of Philadelphia project,

International Aerospace Alliance,

cross-section of implant device,

Reichian Orgastic-type programming

the Psi-Corps,

Alien soul-trading,

Montauk and A-liens from Antares

Leverons...

US Govt and the Greys,

153

Reptoid electronic life support systems

of the Reptoid Humanoids,

new life form masses over the poles

AIDS and Fort Detrick (NSA),

Maglev trains and the US underground

missing human genes,

buried spacecraft and

alien technical archives under Giza pyramid,

the coming new money,

the Black Nobility,

Nordic and human copper based blood systems

technology of cloning and

development of synthetic humans and

political replacement programs, the

Middle East situation,

Congressional awareness of drug and alien agenda,

the MIB,

US Army and helicopter forces,

Govt mobile mind disruption technology,

nature and purpose of the Orion Group,

fourth density transmutation of the human race,

geological changes,

Sirian Mind Control technology,

--as well asillustrations gleaned from witnesses with photographic memory and a lot of courage.

Again, in reference to serpent races, John A. Keel, in his book *Our Haunted Planet'* (1968. Fawcett Publications., Greenwich, Conn.) has stated:

The parahuman Serpent People of the past are still among us. They were probably worshipped by the builders of Stonehenge and the forgotten ridge-making cultures of South America.

In some parts of the world the Serpent People successfully posed as gods and imitated techniques of the super- intelligence. This led to the formation of pagan religions centered around human sacrifices. The conflict, so far as man himself was concerned, became one of religions and races. Whole civilizations based upon the worship of these false gods rose and fell in Asia, Africa, and South America. The battleground had been chosen, and the mode of conflict had been decided upon.

The human race would supply the pawns. The mode of control was complicated as usual. Human beings were largely free of direct control. Each individual had to consciously commit himself to one of the opposing forces. . . . The main battle was for what was to become known as the human soul.

Once an individual had committed himself, he opened a door so that an indefinable something could actually enter his body and exercise some control over his subconscious mind.

(According to Judeo-Christian teaching, THIS would either be the incorruptable Spirit of the Messiah or the soul-destroying spirit of anti-Christ, the serpent, Satan, etc. Just as nature hates a vacuum, so does the human soul and spirit.) What Keel is saying is that the human spirit cannot work entirely of its own volition, but must serve as a channel or a vessel of a higher power, whether that power is good or evil.

The act of free will which is given to man is a choice over which of these powers to submit to or serve, and to accept personal responsibility for that choice. It is the greatest presumption to believe that finite beings like ourselves can choose to be neutral in this ancient battle between the Angelic forces of Light and Life, and the fallen demoniacal powers of Darkness and Death. Neither side will allow for neutral territory, in this case human souls, because the stakes in this Cosmic Conflict are too high - *Branton*).

The Serpent People or OMEGA Group, attacked man in various ways, trying to rid the planet of him. But the super-intelligence was still able to look over man. . . . God worked out new ways of communication and control, always in conflict with the Serpent People.

The mysterious government insider whose books have been published by Tim Beckley's Abelard Press of New York, "Commander X," related a very interesting incident which involved the subterranean mega-complex beneath Dulce, New Mexico. The story he tells might turn out to be an important part of the overall puzzle in connection with that which has previously been related.

One of the many accounts concerning this particular alien stronghold—an underground empire which is apparently attempting to spread it's borders to the Mojave, where they have met resistance from relatively more benevolent human forces -- was related by this anonymous Intelligence Worker, who states:

In another case an old illustrator, John D., does very painstaking work, but during his being on active duty at Dulce he began to act very queerly. He would write letters to the President informing him of a plot underway to undermine the government, and to sabotage the base. He began to draw pictures of American flags, beautifully executed. He drew strange designs of mechanical devices, began to visit the library and bring back books on physics and advanced electronics. He hardly knew how to spell the words.

He would patiently explain something of a very technical nature which he shouldn't have understood. When asked what he was raving about and why he was causing trouble by writing the President, John D. would say that he had been 'sensitized.'

Source Ray White. We do not know its original source, other than the apparent fact that the information seems to be based on the revelations of a certain abductee, and begins by making reference to the Greys as being:

". . . Eaters of souls -- harvest(ers) of souls -- placed in huge globular depositories -- something extracted, as hemoglobin is extracted from blood -- some residue buried in a graveyard not on this planet... couldn't move or speak -- couldn't move head -- tunnel vision -- everything blurred except straight ahead -- they have rank -- like an army but not the same -- you know by the way they 'talk' to each other -- thumb, 3 fingers, perhaps 1 very small -- suction pads on tips of fingers -- our eyes do not pick up the real color of their skin, only a color-blind person would see their skin as it really is -- she saw them as grayish green -- their skin is not their true skin -- it is like a shield they use, a protective covering

(Note: In a similar manner Kenneth Ring, PH,D. in his book, **The Omega Project**, -- William Morrow & Co., N.Y. 1972., states that, based on abductee reports, the 'opaque black' eyes of most of the Greys may also be artificial 'coverings' - *Branton*)

Their perception of pain is different from ours -- one had compassion others did not -- ship blended into rock -- total camouflage – have instruments that can camouflage ships as Army vehicles -- when she entered the ship, at first she thought that she was going into a cave in the rocks -- they take off your clothes right away, without your realizing they have done it -- they have a section strictly for men, another strictly for women -- they did not understand her menstruating -- she had to explain menstrual periods to female alien -- cure of cancer in spices and roots -- deformed babies in some sort of liquid -- some E.T., some human, some E.T./human, some deformed baby animals -- failed experiments -- they have not yet had luck in interbreeding with us -- offspring survive a certain amount of time, but then die -- their metal different from ours, soft but not soft (?) -- they don't understand how we bruise so easily, the softness of our skin -- they were interested in soft spot at top of skull -- they told her about her family history, going way back, ALWAYS the terrible things, traumatic childhood memories, few seconds each, the things she had blocked out, NEVER the happy memories -- they can't understand why we aren't more advanced than they are -- we limit ourselves -- block knowledge out -- ringing in ears both on and off ship -- calf alive but frozen -- different types of samples of animal life -- they give birth through naval, not vagina -- UBAN -- Starmaster 12' tall -- Night of Lights when everyone will see it -- the whole world.

(Note: In most cases the only Greys described as having 'compassion' are the so-called 'hybrids', most of which are actually humans conceived from human semen and ova taken from abductees, yet which have been 'genetically altered' through bio-technology and/or artificial post- natal gene-spicing with the 'A-liens' or other life-forms. Just as the Greys are allegedly part of a lower saurioid hierarchy, the 'hybrids' or 'hubrids' are reportedly the slave-workers who work under them - *Branton*)

Quoting from Commander X--

...From my own intelligence work within the military, I can say with all certainty that one of the main reasons the public has been kept in total darkness about the reality of UFOs and 'A-liens', is that the truth of the matter actually exists too close to home to do anything about. *How could a spokesman for the Pentagon dare admit that five or ten thousand feet underground exists an entire world that is foreign to a belief system we have had for centuries? How could, for example, our fastest bomber be any challenge to those aerial invaders when we can only guess about the routes they take to the surface; eluding*

159

radar as they fly so low, headed back to their underground lair?

Greys and EBEs have established a fortress, spreading out to other parts of the U.S. via means of a vast underground tunnel system that has physically existed since before our recorded history.

Why would the controllers use the United States as the major target of their activity? We believe that this is due to the fact that the United States is a place that was originally intended by it's 'founding fathers' to be a refuge for peoples from all nations to come and work out their collective destinies free from the restrictions of prejudice and dictatorial or tyrannical rule -- a land where all people could express their creativity and individual destinies without interferance. This was their intention; however, it is obvious that the dream has not been fully realized because collective and governmental compromize of the principle that all men are created equal.

There is even the possibility presented by some accounts that Sauroids & Reptoids themselves have their own chameleon-like (human-appearing) representatives walking among us, infiltrating our society, for the most part unknown for their true nature among human leadership. Examples of "Reptilian" Elites abound among hoarding and cavorting Billionaire$: Windsors, Rothschilds, Rockefellers and Kissinger are among those pretending to be human.

We have mentioned a few cases previously, however there is another account of a 'chameleon' entity [who remains nameless] who may have attempted to infiltrate the

Pentagon itself in an effort to seize information about U.S. plans for 'Star Wars' or SDI technology.

The unconfirmed account alleged that such a person was in fact apprehended after a contact lense he was wearing while posing as a high military officer fell out, revealing a strange eye-arrangement and a verticaly-slit pupil. The man was apprehended and studied, and he found to possess a Reptoid internal makeup! His apartment where he was staying was searched and numerous copies of sensitive documents relating to SDI were discovered within—data he was going to send to his superiors.

The U.S. appears to be in essence a World Scenario, if not a universal scenario in miniature and therefore, the Conspiracy sees it as a most valuable prize. It would probably not be too far out to suggest that the war between the human and serpent races from all three realms converges in the United States and, to be more exact, within the vicinities of Mt. Archuleta near Dulce, New Mexico (the major earth-base of the Reptoid Empire); the Panamint Mountains of California (the major earth-base of the Nordic Federation); and the real hotbed of inner-planetary and cyber-electronic warfare, the Nevada Test Site.

During the contactee era of the late 1950's and early '60's a man by the name of Mel Noel made the rounds of the UFO circuit describing his experiences as an Air Force 'line pilot' whose top secret mission involved the photographing of UFO's (both visible and 'cloaked' craft -- radar directing and infrared film being used for the latter). These encounters usually took place over the Rocky mountains of Utah and Idaho, according to Noel, and throughout the years

1953-54. One of Noel's lectures was delivered during that period to a huge crowd at the Giant Rock UFO Convention held in the Mojave desert near Twenty Nine Palms, California.

For several years 'Mel Noel' was out of the news, until in the early 1990's that is, when he reappeared stating that 'Noel' was merely a pseudonym, and implyed that because of greater present-day awareness of UFO phenomena he could more easily use his real name of 'Guy Kirkwood'. Kirkwood later appeared on the premier 'UFO Contact' episode of the Fox Networks 'Sightings' series, in the early 1990's. Kirkwood described an almost identical account as was given by Noel.

Kirkwood's (or 'Noel's') commanding officer during the operation had allegedly established radio contact with the human occupants of alien craft, who were rather attractive in appearance and could even pass themselves off as Americans if they were to walk the streets of any large city. His Commanding Officer later claimed that he had physical contacts with these craft. These human-like A-liens claimed during a radio conversation (between themselves and the Commanding Officer -- a conversation which Noel and his three co-pilots were allowed to listen in on) that they were from underground cities beneath other planetary bodies in the Sol System, as well as from underground cities within the earth itself. They claimed that these colonies or societies were affiliated together through a Central 'Tribunal' on or below the moons of Saturn. In Kirkwood's own words, in reference to this communication:

...They referred to, they made the statement that our scientists had made statements based upon theories that life cannot and therefore does not exist ON the other planets in this system, and they said that they were confirming those statements. he said, 'life does not and cannot exist ON these other planets; it's all **inside** the planets, it's all **in the interior,** just as "the house of the Lord." this is the House of the Lord we live in--the interior of the planet. (Likewise, it is the interior of the Moon, Mars & Mercury that is inhabited, not the exterior.--Editor.)

In connection with the subject of this File, that is the 'invasion' of an alien race from above and below utilizing mind-bending techniques, psychological warfare, mind control and implantation, we will quote from Brad Steiger's *'The UFO Abductors'* (1988., Berkley Books., N.Y.):

Dr. Clifford Wilson [M.A., B.D., Ph.D.], in his book *"UFOS... and Their Mission Impossible"* (Signet Books., N.Y.) presents his own intelligence or research concerning the on- going invasion/ infiltration of our society by alien powers:

"...Not only have many seen UFOs, but there is also a growing army of those who claim to have had actual contact with UFO occupants. An authoritative, and possibly conservative, estimate is that there are 50,000 silent contactees in the United States alone.

"It could well be there are thousands of people who do have information and are not prepared to reveal it because of threatened consequences to themselves. Possibly many do not know they have that knowledge because they themselves gained it in a hypnotic state.

163

"Hypnotized Slaves Await a Signal? - Nations could be conquered by the infiltration of agents into government seats of authority, and it is surely more frightening to think that mankind could be overcome and even destroyed by programmed men and women from within their own ranks. If there is indeed a final confrontation approaching, an army of people could be involved. They could be ready to take action which they themselves do not even anticipate, but yet with no option but to obey because they have been conditioned to obey, at a given signal."

We are not alone in suggesting this dreadful possibility. To quote John Keel once again:

We have no way of knowing how many human beings throughout the world have been processed in this manner, since they would have absolutely no memory of undergoing the experience, and so we have no way of determining who among us has strange and sinister 'programs' lying dormant in the dark corners of his mind.

Suppose a plan is to process millions of people and then at some future date trigger all of those minds at one time? Would we suddenly have a world of saints? Or would we have a world of armed maniacs shooting at one another from bell towers?

A Frightening Prospect.--If there is some great super- plan of a spiritual counterattack to reach its culmination in Armageddon, it could well be that (this) army of slaves will be available to obey orders, without even knowing beforehand that they have been inducted into the armed forces of what the Bible refers to as the principalities and powers.

164

This sort of activity has followed many other supposed saucer sightings. The similarities between the stories are of such a nature as to cause surprise at first -- someone temporarily in a trance, men posing as air force or other officials, those men being slight in stature with dark olive skins and pointed features, and the contactees having dreadful headaches, hallucinations, and nightmares. Some of them have gone into trances and have temporarily become mediums through whom strange voices could be heard...

On July 30, 1992, radio announcer and reporter for **Radio Free America**, Anthony J. Hilder, sent the following letter to Patty Cafferata., Lincoln County District Attorney., Pioche, Nevada 89043. Several dozen copies were sent by Hilder to other researchers as well as several activist, political, legal, media, patriot, congressional, and (real) 'National Defense' officials:

"Dear Mrs. Cafferata: I am calling on the Attorney General of the State of Nevada to initiate an immediate 'full scale' Grand Jury Investigation into the activities of the Wackenhut S.S., your office and the Lincoln County Sheriff's Department. The reason for the urgency of this action is because of the rapidly increasing number of 'life threatening' situations created by unidentified paramilitary personnel who operate under the color of law to harass, intimidate and suppress the constitutional rights of many hundreds of American citizens and Japanese nationals who come to view the Unidentified Flying 'Saucer-Shaped Disks' being tested over your county.

"It is my prayer that with the prodding of the people and the press that the Attorney General will launch 'this

165

investigation' in time to avert one of these innocent individuals from being murdered by that paramilitary mob or winding up as a permanent prisoner in one of the 'strange' underground 'experimental laboratories' below Dreamland and S-4 within the Nellis Test Range.

"During my conversation with you on the afternoon of June 6, I made repeated attempts to acquire the names of six individuals who were arrested last month by the Lincoln County Sheriff's Department somewhere in the Tickaboo Valley. As a reporter, I sought your professional cooperation. I did not get it.

"Not only did you refuse to reveal the names of those arrested and their 'alleged' violation of law -- you continually badgered me for my home address, phone number and specifically just what radio stations would be broadcasting the story. Could it be that you wanted to 'cover-up' the story? As I stated, I simply wanted to cover the event.

"I am curious as to the reason you would attempt to prevent the media from reporting the arrest. Obviously you didn't want me to contact those people for their side of the story before their arraignment. Is there something you fear from honest disclosure? What is it that you don't want to know? Could it be that these arrests were illegal?

"Did the Sheriff's Department violate Constitutional rights' of these citizens, Mrs. Cafferata? Has it become the policy of Lincoln County Sheriff's Department WITH YOUR APPROVAL and under the color of law, to 'HARASS AND INTIMIDATE' the curious onlookers who come to your county to sit beneath the stars in the high desert, hoping to see and possibly photograph the strange and 'alien lights' in the night sky for which that region has now become famous? Is this a crime in Nevada? One might wonder if Lincoln has now become the first county in a 'Hitlerian Superstate' of a NEW WORLD ORDER -- where freedoms are suppressed and terror tactics are 'public policy'?

"...It's definitely not a TOP SECRET that what's going on within the bowels of those underground bunkers at S-4 and Area 51 in the Nellis Test Site is 'ABOVE TOP SECRET'. Obviously there's something very strange going on out there that the 'BLACK PROJECT BOYS' have to hide regardless of what it costs. If the public were to become aware of what these 'Dr. Strangelove's' were 'creating' in those underground laboratories -- I believe the world would be shocked and horrified beyond all belief.

"Need I remind you that it is your responsibility as District Attorney of Lincoln County to UNCOVER -- NOT COVER UP crimes that are being committed in your county. Other questions arise. Is there a dereliction of duty by the District Attorney's office? Do you have a conflict of interest? And for whom do you serve?

"I am deeply concerned as is the American Civil Liberties Union in seeing that the constitutional rights of all Americans who live in or pay a visit to Lincoln County are PROTECTED -- NOT VIOLATED by the WACKENHUT S.S. (Security Service), your Sheriff's Department, or anyone else.

"Correct me if I am wrong, but at one time or another did you not take some sort of oath to uphold and defend the Constitution of the United States? Or is the

167

Lincoln County District Attorney EXEMPT from upholding such 'antiquated trivialities' as the United States Constitution?

"Would you be willing to share with me information as to how and why the Wackenhut S.S. is ALLOWED by your office under the color of law to STOP, INTIMIDATE AND HARASS 'sightseers' on PUBLIC land? Are they 'ABOVE THE LAW'? Are they IMMUNE TO PROSECUTION? . . . "

" . . . Of course there's a difference between Bush and Hitler's phraseology. Hitler talked about a THOUSAND-YEAR REICH. Bush talks about a THOUSAND POINTS OF LIGHT.

"I know it's very hard for you to accept, even in your wildest thoughts, that an American Auschwitz could exist undereAmerican soil. I bet it's even harder for you to conceive that it could be fully functioning in Lincoln County. Are you willing to testify in a court of law that it doesn't exist there, Mrs. Cafferata?

Those that asked local government officials, like yourself, what is going on were told that it was all TOP SECRET and involved national security . . . and not to question Authority. Then one day when the war came to a close and the truth was unearthed, the 'party people' acted shocked when it became public that millions had been mass-murdered. They just couldn't believe that genocide, infanticide and homicide could have been not only allowed but carried out to the last deadly detail by other 'party liners' in the government **who just went along...... saw nothing, said nothing and did nothing. . . .**

I am not accusing you of any crime, Mrs. Cafferata. It is possible that you could just be so inordinately apathetic or just so blindly obeying orders that you cannot see, or simply refuse to open your eyes to what's going on. Or do you 'CLAIM INNOCENCE', Mrs. Cafferata? The Attorney General's office will be the judge of that. It is the A.G.'s responsibility to determine if any crimes have been, or are now being committed or allowed 'to be committed' by your office. Ultimately, any decision with regards to the 'wholesale abuse of the law' is made by the prosecution who tries the case, be it in a court of law or before the bar of public opinion...

Sincerely, Anthony J. Hilder – *Radio Free America*

The United States of Inc.

SECTION 8: the 2000s -:-

a NEW AGE OF TRUTH

INVESTIGATORS INTO DISAPPEARANCES

Off. David Paulides, Dr. Karla Turner, Ph.D., Off. Bruce Witkowsky,

INTO SECRET SPACE PROGRAMS

Dan Burisch, Ph.D., Steven Greer, M.D., Charles Hall, Gary McKinnon, Michael Salla, Ph.D.;

INTO HISTORY

Zecharia Sitchin, Lloyd Pye, Michael Tellinger, VLKudin

INTO COSMOLOGY AND CLIMATOLOGY

Loren Moret, Michael Janitch, Erik Dubay

Much damage to our ecosystem has accrued. Ozone depletion & the unstable weather patterns are rapidly endangering life on our planet. Alternatives include - 1) direct handling of the atmospheric problems, 2) taking shelter in underground domains, & 3) escape to other planetary bodies in the solar system, have been devised in secret.

Based upon relatively elusive yet extensive accounts and relative data which has been gathered by a loosely-connected group of researchers, we can conclude that the subterranean network--whatever it consists of presently--is basically inhabited by both human and non-human Reptoid beings. In those areas where humans are not being controlled by non-humans or Saurians, there is obviously conflict between the two races as foretold in Genesis chapter 3.

Evidence suggesting a secret project to fly 'alien' vehicles in Nevada to Alien/US/Soviet bases and operations on the Moon are now some of the hot topics amongst UFOlogists and researchers. These are, for most people, ideas that are so far out that they cannot be believed. One reasons for this attitude is the fact that VERY few people have ever researched anything having to do with the U.S. OFFICIAL space program, NASA, and it's relationship to the UFO coverup. If researchers, authors, lecturers, etc., would take the time to point out where NASA has suppressed, hidden and simply lied about information dealing with the U.S. space program people may consider these esoteric ideas more believable based on their new knowledge that the U.S. space program is not what it appears to be.

Moongate by William Brian II is a good place to start. After that you can talk to people at NASA. Specifically people connected with the Department of Defense (DOD) missions. Many of these people, if willing to talk, will paint a very different picture of what is happening with OUR space program (remember, it is a civilian operation right??? Well, if you think it is, you had better look again).

NASA was created on October 1, 1958. The main reason for NASA's creation was to capitalize on the military potential of space. A secondary reason was so that large sums of money may be diverted into 'black' projects which the public was to have no knowledge about. The plan was simple and quite easily accomplished. Money and manu-factured items for top-secret or black projects can readily be allocated if they are hidden within our unclassified projects.

Contractors and Subcontractors brought in by NASA have no idea where the money goes, what the parts they design and manufacture are really for and they almost never see the end project or result because everything is so compartmentalized at NASA.

I am still in the process of gathering, verifying, and assembling this information ,so naturally I am interested in finding others who may be able to support or refute any of my findings. The following list of facts I have learned from several individuals who are working or who have worked or been linked with NASA in some way over the years. For obvious reasons I will not now use their real names.

The list below represents some of the information from three people: one is currently working in DOD missions for NASA; another started working with NASA & DOD when JSC (Johnson Space Center) was built. He 'committed suicide' after the Space Shuttle Challenger was destroyed. "The third is a scientist who has worked at NASA and other facilities. His work with Edward Teller *(i.e. the inventor of the H-Bomb and alleged member of MJ-12 - Branton)* is what is most known about this man:

"* There are buildings, equipment, paths and glass canopies on the Moon.

"* Photos—NASA photos—exist which clearly civil and mechanical artifacts.

"* Hndreds, but probably thousands, of NASA photos have been tampered with as to orientation, scaling, contrast and colors. Moreover, by careful use of an airbrush, flying saucers and other UFOs are removed, and then the photo is released to the public and/or press.

"* Film taken by astronauts clearly show UFOs, IFOs, and content which is not discussed in NASA accompanying text.

"* The NSA screens all photos before release to the public.

"* Everything that NASA has launched has been closely monitored by at least one 'alien' culture.

"* NASA knew about 'alien' activity on the Moon before Armstrong, Aldrin, and Collins ever set foot on it.

"* 'Buzz' Aldrin had a nervous breakdown because of these events and the pressure not to talk.

"* Certain 'Ham' radio operators have allegedly recorded conversations from 'classified' frequencies between a Space Shuttle astronaut and Mission Control, making reference to an 'Alien Craft' which was following the Shuttle.

"* There have been 22 deaths (many 'suicides') at JSC in Houston.

"* The Space Station project is non-existent. It is a lie and will never be built. In reality the project is called the Space City.

"* No astronaut who has seen AVs or ETs is allowed to talk about it, even amongst themselves. If they do and are caught they may be fined, publicly humiliated, imprisoned, or have all pensions and future salaries taken away.

"* Voyager was disabled. The pictures received from 'Neptune' in September of 1989 were not from the probe.

"* Galileo has been put out of commission and will not be allowed to complete its mission. The Secret Government loaded Galileo with several pounds of plutonium, which 'they' intended to use to ignite the hydrogenic 'atmosphere' of Jupiter and thus create a nuclear reaction which would theoretically convert Jupiter into a small binary 'sun' and call the new star 'Lucifer', as a SIGN announcing the 'New World Order'.

"...A Soviet scientist who defected to the West said photographs taken by an orbiting satellite clearly show the ruined temples of a long-dead civilization - on the planet Mars!

"And LASER PROBES made by the secret Russian satellite revealed that the ruins littering the planet's surface ARE incredibly new by space-time standards.

"The 58-year-old scientist was a high-echelon member of an elite team that has worked together since 1961 when Vostok 1 carried Yuri A. Gagarin as the first man in space. "But Russia's growing emphasis on the development of a nuclearized 'Star Wars' satellite system in space prompted him to flee Russia. He now lives under an assumed identity somewhere in Switzerland."

There is a medical-pharmaceutical fifth column in this country that is tied up with A-liens. Selenium is being slipped into SULFA DRUGS, and this selenium lodges in the bones and makes the body receptive to extremely short waves, those in the wave band of the brain. Similar to the waves that can be detected by the encephalograph. About 300,000 people in this country have been sensitized by ingestion of selenium; and at least seven secret radio stations have been set up in this country, and they are broadcasting to these sensitized persons, instructing them in the best way to perform acts of sabotage against our planet.'

There is a movement underway to bring the minds of the masses under the subjection of some alien force, whether through implantation or other means, and that these alien powers from all indications intend on bringing humanity under their control through such manipulations. These broadcasts are received by sensitized and sensitive individuals, this Editor among them. And knowing what is being broadcast is one way to disarm it.

Regarding NASA & MARS.--"Thirty scientists known as the Mars Investigation Group, think two photographs sent back from Mars in 1976 by the Viking space-probe indicate the existence of an ancient civilization, said Richard Hoagland, group member and science writer.

"The photos show what appear to be four huge pyramids lined up symmetrically with the face about 6 miles away, suggesting a parallel with Stonehenge, the ancient monument of huge stones in England, Hoagland said Thursday. . . . "'Geometrically, the face could be seen in profile [from the pyramids] as the summer solstice sun rose over it.'

NASA treachery and malfeasance serves as a reminder that policy and dogma do not need to represent any Truth as we know what "being true" is about.

Why DOES NASA Lie?

The crew of the Challenger have been located. If ANY one of these people are the same as the ones in the "spacecraft", then it didn't explode with a crew inside, now did it? How can these people have died and all these crew members still be alive? Because it never happened. You only think it did because "NASA said so and showed you a nice explosion on TV.

THE UNITED NATIONS TODAY

"Not only does the Charter Organization NOT BY LAW prevent future wars, but it makes it practically certain that we shall have future wars, and as such wars it takes from us (The United States) the power to declare them, to chose the

176

side on which we shall fight, to determine what forces and military equipment we shall use in the war, and to control and command our sons who do the fighting. "In fact, A Soviet General in the United Nations still writes the plans for employment of United States troops all over the world, even in the Persian Gulf today.

As all masonic Secret Societies operate, Leftist guerrillas think they are at the top of the Ladder, never realizing that there were higher-ups over them. Those who earn the wrath of the Rothschilds, mercens operate oligarchy, Fascism and Globalism with impunity. Actually, as it turns out, THEY (the secret societies) are now being dominated' by Other Worlders.

Be that as it may, the current doctrine of Federal policy vis a vis Extra-terrestrials staps back and lets them do what they want. "Since our weapons were literally useless against A-liens, Majesty Twelve decided to continue friendly diplomatic relations until such a time as we were able to develop a technology which would enable us to challenge them on a military bases. Overtures would have to be made to the Soviet Union and other nations to join forces for the survival of humanity. In the meantime Plans were developed to research and construct two weapons systems using conventional and nuclear technology, which would hopefully bring us to parity.

The Strange Story of J-Rod, An EBE, by Linda
Moulton Howe, Source:Earth Files
http://earthfiles.com/earth043.html

When I first heard Bill Uhouse, a retired mechanical
engineer from Las Vegas, tell his story of having been
involved in reverse engineering alien technology at certain
government facilities, I was both amused and bemused. I
was amused because he indicated that the big boss of the
project was an extraterrestrial biological entity that he knew
as J-Rod who was supposed to have arrived on earth in
1953. According to another source called BJ discussed
further in this article, the " J"and "Rod" were derived from
early attempts to establish communication between the
extraterrestrial biological entity, EBE, and U. S. scientists
privy to EBE contact. Since the release of the MJ-12
Eisenhower Briefing Document in the early 1980s, the term
EBE has come into popular use to designate diminutive,
grey-colored humanoids associated with crashed saucers.
Another variant spelling is Eben used by physicist Paul
Bennewitz and others. Some implied that Ebens also were a
class of EBEs with certain distinct physical characteristics
and were said to be working with our military scientists and
engineers on various projects. According to BJ, no language

interface with the EBE existed in 1953, so a series of symbols were shown to test his reactions. Some symbols looked like letters and others were geometric shapes. The first symbol the EBEN pointed to looked like a "J." The other was an "inertial-bar" that looked like a rod. So, humans called the Eben "J-Rod." I was bemused because I wondered why he was disclosing information concerning a highly classified operation and was also skeptical about another "insider" with tales about Area 51 and S-4.

Kingman, Arizona (Background)

Engineer Bill Uhouse claims there was a crash of an Eben aerial craft near Kingman, Arizona in 1953 and that four entities survived. That would have been six years after the more famous Roswell crashes and retrievals of "interplanetary craft of unknown origin." In Kingman, according to Uhouse, two disabled Ebens and two more that were in good condition were retrieved by U. S. Government units specially trained for retrieval missions. The two non-humans in good condition were allowed to re-enter the craft and the disabled entities were taken to an unspecified medical facility. He also states that a recovery crew that entered the craft to inspect it came down with a mysterious sickness. The craft was then loaded aboard a trailer and hauled off to the Nevada Test Site north of Las Vegas. Bill Uhouse claims that the events at Kingman eventually resulted in the project which employed him to design and construct a flight simulator that ourairmen could use to learn how to fly a saucer. Bill claims that he met one of the A-liens who apparently supervised this project and was known as J-Rod . Bill says he worked both at Los Alamos and Area 51. Bill tells a fascinating story and it would have remained just a story until I read about a document that purported to be a technical paper on tissue samples taken from an EBE known as AQ-J-ROD. BJ says the "AQ" signifies Project Aquarius under the Majestic-12 group created by U. S. President Harry S. Truman in 1947 and assigned to research the crashed disc and non-human bodies that had descended upon the United States in the 1940's.

2002 Gary McKinnon, UK

McKinnon was an amateur hacker

who logged on to NASA and was

able to access this department. They had huge, high-resolution images stored in their picture files presumably taken by a satellite looking down on it. Objects didn't look manmade or anything like what we have. At his crowning moment, someone at NASA discovered what he was doing and disconnected. He also got access to Excel spreadsheets. One was titled "Non-Terrestrial Officers." It contained names and ranks of U.S. Air Force personnel who are not registered anywhere else. It also contained information about ship-to-ship transfers, but I've never seen the names of these ships noted anywhere else. For these crimes he was held in danger of extradition and long-term imprisonment for several years, until a UK judge blocked US extradiction.

Tall Whites & Charles Hall from **Michael E. Salla**, PhD, December 16, 2004

This takes me to the final issue which concerns <u>Charles</u> response that the Tall Whites can't be restricted in any way by the USAF. He believes that it is suicidal to try to restrict the Tall Whites , and that only carefully negotiated agreements can be made with them. This is reminiscent of the comments by **Col Phillip Corso** that the US had entered into a kind of 'negotiated surrender' <u>with an extraterrestrial race</u>:

"We had negotiated a kind of surrender with them [extraterrestrials] as long as we couldn't fight them. They dictated the terms because they knew what we most feared was disclosure" (<u>The Day After Roswell</u>, p.292).

Hall certainly believes, along with the US military, that the Tall White's technological superiority forces the US military to enter into agreements that may not reflect very favorable terms.

In Hall's <u>Millennial Hospitality</u>, a revealing passage describes the extent to which Tall Whites want to instill in Charles a sense of their technological superiority and the ineffectiveness of any offensive measures (vol II, pp. 274-

75). Charles is told to throw a rock at a Tall White guard and reluctantly complies only to witness it being stopped in mid-flight, along with other rocks that were thrown.

Such a display of technological superiority was intended to impress on Charles, and presumably on the USAF, the failure of any kind of attack on the Tall Whites' society. However, rather than demonstrate Tall Whites' technical superiority, doesn't this act of bravado achieve the very opposite? *Doesn't it reveal that the Tall Whites are perhaps **too eater to impress Charles and the USAF** with the futility of any kind of attack on them ?* This eagerness most likely comes not from a sense of invulnerability, but from a perceived weakness that they are intending to hide.

It has been speculated by remote viewer **Ingo Swann** that *extraterrestrial races with advanced technologies are actually quite vulnerable to the advanced psychic abilities of humans* (**Penetration: The Question of Extraterrestrial and Human Telepathy**, 1998).

If it is accurate that the *Tall Whites feel vulnerable* to some human potential that might threaten them, then it may be that psychic abilities are what the Tall Whites fear, rather than US military technology. If this is the case, then that might explain why **Charles Hall** has been allowed to come forward and reveal to the general public his remarkable contact experiences while serving in the **USAF**.

If **Tall Whites** are engaging in resource extraction from Earth on terms that US military and/or the 'shadow government' is unhappy with but feels unable to change, then the US ilitary/Shadow government may be looking for some way to change the terms of their agreements. If Swann and others are correct about human psychic abilities and the potential of human consciousness, then releasing this information to the general public may be a means of introducing global consciousness as a factor in what has been happening secretly.

Charles Hall reveals important details about the nature of agreements between US government/military authorities and the *Tall Whites*. Resource extraction that is occurring may be nothing more than a benign exchange of food, clothes and metals for the advanced technology being supplied by Tall Whites. IF, on the other hand, a more sinister extraction of Earth resources is taking place—then what may be involved is *relocation of those being* fed and clothed by USAF material supplies, against the wishes of our Guests who feel powerless to prevent it.

Whatever the truth concerning resource extraction that is happening, what is important is that the general public become informed of what is in such secret trade agreements, and we the People must by Law ensure that such ET-transactions are marked by transparency, accountability and thrift. Trade agreements with the **Tall Whites must reflect mutual quid pro quo demonstrations of Trust, as with any** technologically advanced <u>extra-terrestrial race</u>.

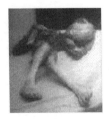

J-Rod, Technical Adviser,

183

Nevada Test Site

On visits to the flight simulator, Bill Uhouse would occasionally see who acted as a technical adviser to the ultra-secret program that Bill worked on. It was J-Rod, a typical gray-colored EBE, hairless and without facial expressions. He had large, black wrap-around eyes or eye-lenses that are typical of these creatures. He is reported to be 200 years old, suffering from cell deterioration and still located at Papoose S-4, Area 51 in Nevada. But I can't confirm that. According to Bill Uhouse, the funny thing was how he dressed in human trousers and a loose shirt. His shoes were different, but I don't know in what way. His four-finger hands were long.

The Dan Burisch Report, 2004-2005

On April 11, 2005, an affidavit was submitted to the Canadian Federal Court on behalf of an asylum application by Don Deppeller concerning harassment over his investigations of whistleblower claims made by Dr Dan Burisch. The affidavit was publicly signed by Dan Burisch and photographed where both Burisch and the affidavit can be viewed HERE. In the affidavit, Burisch has confirmed many of the allegations made by Deppeller that he was placed under surveillance in the United States as a result of his activities to verify the details of the Dan Burisch story. Consequently, Deppeller felt compelled to leave the U.S. for Canada in early 2003 and eventually filed for asylum.

The affidavit is significant since Burisch for the first time has testified in a legal process over his alleged involvement in a number of classified projects. This gives support to earlier interviews involving Burisch where he allegedly was

184

prepared to testify before Congress on the nature of his classified activities (see HERE.) In an interview on the Jeff Rense show on April 14, 2005, Deppeller outlined the nature of his investigations of the Burisch saga and why he initiated an asylum application in Canada.

Dan Burisch claims to be a microbiologist who worked on a number of highly classified projects including one that presumably provides a means for creating life - Project Lotus. Burisch allegedly interacted with an extraterrestrial called J-Rod and as a consequence has been able to pioneer some breakthroughs into a mysterious molecule called the Ganesh particle that provides the solution to how to generate life. As a result of his highly classified work in Project Lotus and other projects, Burisch has allegedly become privy to how a variety of secret committees operate to control extraterrestrial affairs.

The two main committees are the MJ-12 Group originally formed to deal with the extraterrestrial phenomenon; and an international committee called the Committee of the Majority formed in the 1960s as result of international efforts led by the Soviet Union to more widely disseminate extraterrestrial technologies to the international community. For an article summarizing the Burisch see: Exo-Comment-12

What makes the Burisch Affidavit, and his case more generally, absorbing for many of those investigating his claims is the perspective that Burisch is allegedly aware of an Extinction Level Event (ELE) coming towards the Earth in the 2012 time frame. In the affidavit he states:

Some implications of these projects ... are of such a grave nature that, were the general world human population to know the entirety of the information contained within them, the resultant reactions of portions of the present human population may vary from "no reaction" to potential 'panic'.

This event which threatens to kill off 90% of the human population is apparently the driving rationale for why disclosure of the extraterrestrial presence and associated information has not occurred.

According to an interview Burisch had with long time UFO researcher, Bill Hamilton, this ELE is associated with some kind of "convergent time line paradox" where humanity splits in two after the ELE, and from this two groups of extraterrestrials are involved. One is the 'Zeta Reticulums' or 'J-Rods' who are physically degenerated humans from the future. The other are Nordic looking humans from Orion who are the descendents of humans able to survive the ELE in the future (see HERE). In the affidavit, Burisch states that there has been a treaty signed between the clandestine government authorities and the extraterrestrials in order to fully deal with the consequences of the forthcoming ELE event that generates two separate branches of humanity in the future:

"You have also been a party during the negotiations of a treaty known as the "Tau-9 Conference for the Preservation of Humanity", between present human authorities and certain individuals representing themselves as extraterrestrial peoples, with their origin alleged to you as the star

186

constellations "Reticulum" and "Orion." You have had physical interaction with at least one such extraterrestrial."

Burisch and Deppeller describe the Nordics as benevolent and very spiritual which is very consistent with the many 'contacteé reports' that began in the 1950's (see HERE). In contrast the Reticulums/J-Rods have two factions. One is friendly to humanity and wishes to assist in coming up with solutions to the forthcoming 2012 ELE. The other is unfriendly and is seeking to take whatever advantage it can be performing widespread abductions and genetic engineering with human population up to 2012. So these three extraterrestrials factions are presumably interacting with humanity and the 'controllers' of extraterrestrial information, MJ-12 in ways which reflect different agendas and priorities.

Burisch claims in his affidavit to have worked directly with MJ-12: "You [Burisch] have been formally associated with the group known as Majestic 12, since 1986, were formally dissociated from the public on June 8, 2004 (then at the instruction of Majestic 12), and were professionally dissociated from Majestic 12, albeit under emeritus status, on March 21, 2005..."

According to Burisch and insiders sympathetic to his efforts to release information, the MJ-12 Group is split on the issue of disclosure. The larger international committee, the Committee of the Majority has apparently been dissolved as a result of conflict between MJ-12 and the larger financial and cultural interests that make up the Committee of the Majority known more generally as the Illuminati.

So what we have then from the Burisch affidavit and other material is a very complex story involving two factions of human controllers (MJ-12 and the Illuminati) and three factions of extraterrestrials (J-Rods -friendly and unfriendly- and Nordic Orions.) This means that events leading up to the ELE in 2012 is a five tiered conflict between actors with different agendas and activities in their interactions with one another, the human population and secret control groups. Apparently, the very future of human life is at stake and supporters of the Burisch material, such as Deppeller advocate preparing for a possible catastrophic event that wipes out 90% of the population.

In the Deppeller interview, Jeff Rense suggests that secret preparation for an ELE is the only thing that can explain the illogical policies of secret controllers (MJ-12 and Committee of the Majority/Illuminati) that are systematically exploiting, abusing and mishandling the global environment and planetary resources. The logic Rense suggests from observing global events, and fully supported by Deppeller's research into the Burisch affair, is that an ELE is highly likely from the perspective of the controllers.

Consequently, disclosure of the extraterrestrial presence needs to be done in a way that doesn't panic the global population over the likelihood of an ELE [in 2012] which has led to the controllers putting in place a process for ensuring continuity of government and survival of the human race.

The "What Shape is the Earth" DISPUTE??

188

Erik Dubay and a plethora of investigators, watchers, seers and counter-counter Red Pillers have gotten into a pissing contest over whether our world is a ball or a pancake with a canopy over it.

Let you just inform you, the state of the discussion is that YOUTUBE has removed ALL—EVERY--SINGLE--video that presents our world as a "plane."

You go from there.

EXT, Wha t is the Stat us of the DU MBs ?

Michael Janitch [Dutchsinse] and many others have been documenting the status and effects of chemtrails, e'quakes, sinkholes, violent storms and other natural phenomena.

However, in 2011, if you can still find references to it, there was a series of 5+ earthquakes in Colorado and Mt Weather, Virginia; and Janitch followed the smoke from underground fires and explosions from the Nuclear Plant north to Dulce, west to 29 Palms, from there north from volcanic vent-to-volcanic-vent all the way up to Washington State. This was while the mainstream media was silent.

What we can infer—what some people inferred—from this underground series of explosions and trailing smoke—was that the DUMBs were under serious attack. My own sources say, half the DUMBs are no longer servicable and large numbers of the human and non-human population underground were annihilated by fire and radioactivity. But of course, official sources are not saying boo.

NIBIRU.

I'll tell you what I know and can show you.

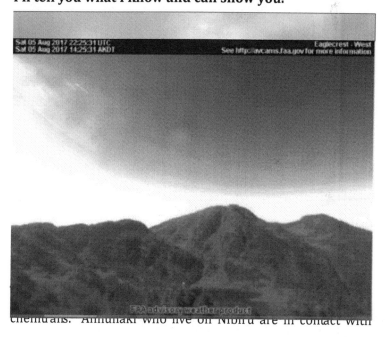

chemtrails. Annunaki who live on Nibiru are in contact with

Tall White and Globalist partisans; but they also have to deal with their own partisans who are more familiar with life on the ground than they are. Enki, Ningishidda, Ereshkigal all took

Red Pills.

Here is the "rim" of Nibiri--close as this, hiding behind chemtrails. Annunaki who live on Nibiru are in contact with Tall White and Globalist partisans; but they also have to deal with their own partisans who are more familiar with life on the ground than they are. Enki, Ningishidda, Ereshkigal all took Red Pills.

THE END GAME WE'RE IN NOW

Some researchers believe that within the deepest levels of the government is an on-going 'covert space program' utilizing some very remarkable aerospace and propulsion technologies. However, the very nature of this program, the clandestine (and possibly illegal) means by which it is funded, as well as the possible means by which they came across this 'technology', has led the 'Secret' Government into keeping activities [along with time travel] a worldclass top secret.

Apparently they have enforced this cover-up, as John Lear says, with 'deadly force'. Perhaps one of the most important reasons for the secrecy, according to some, is that SOME groups within the secret government have allegedly -- in the face of 'superior alien technology' -- 'surrendered' to a malevolent alien race and have become their 'agents' on earth.

Is it also possible -- as many researchers and prominent military, government and industrial personnel confirm -- that the 'secret government' utilizes advanced super-technology (hidden from the public) to carry out a clandestine space program involving manned flight to planets and moons?

George Andrews suspects that 'Starfleet International' consists of human-military personnel only, while the 'United Federated Planets' may somehow tie-in with the non-human entities such as 'Serpent Race' or Greys. However, Andrews' theory that THIS particular Governmental establishment has collaborated with the Greys is yet to be confirmed. See Roster below.

There is evidence in fact that certain 'Constituted Government' officials (who are loyal to the American-Constitutional 'Republic') -- as confirmed by Guy Kirkwood and others -- have secret 'alliances' with the 'Nordics';

192

wheres Secret Government collaborators (who are loyal to the Bavarian Roman 'Empire') tend to collaborate with the Saurian Greys, etc.

Below is a reproduction of the document:

UNITED FEDERATED PLANETS

STARFLEET INTERNATIONAL

U.S.S. CONCORD NCC-1989

CREW ROSTER

crew member	sf expiration	serv. number
Col. Mike Ferguson (sfc st./mc)	june 1990*@	scmc-8901-0002
Lt. Laura Ferguson (sfc)	june 1990@	scm-8901-0007
Lcdr. Harlan Stevens (sfc)	sep. 1989@	scss-8906.23
ens. rebecca burand (sfc)	sep. 1989@	scs-8902-0004
maj. mike west (sfc staff/mc)	ufp only	scmc-8901-0004
lt. katrina caskey (sfc)	nov. 1989@	sce-8906-0005
2lt. bob burrall (sfmc)	nov. 1989@	scmc-8906-0003
cmdr. bob tompkins (sfc)	dec. 1989@	sce-8906-0002
sgm. ray chambers (sfmc)	dec. 1989@	scmc-8903-0008
(x)		
ens. ron caskey (sfc)	jan. 1990@	scsy-0906-0005
lt. debra mcclary (sfc)	jan. 1990@	scss-8906-0004
(x)		
msg. ivan goodman (sfmc)	jan. 1990@	scmc-8904-0001
cs. crystal ferguson (sfc)	an. 1990@	scm-8906-0011
(x)		
mdsm. philippe beaudette (sfc)	jan. 1990@	scm-8906-0009
a-ens. everett new (sfc)	feb. 1990@	sce-8906-0007
msg. john higgins (sfmc)	feb. 1990@	scmc-8906-0010
(x)		
wo3. doug taylor (sfmc)	mar. 1990@	scmc-8906-0001
(x)		
cs. rose taylor (sfc)	mar. 1990@	scs-8906-0012
sp1. amanda taylor (sfc)	mar. 1990@	scmc-8906-0001
(x)		
a-ens. kelly maddox (sfc)	mar. 1990@	scss-8906-0008
radm. anne miller (sfc staff)	may 1990*@	smc-8901-0006
(x)		
ltjg. sharen burrall (sfc)	may 1990@	scss-8906-0014
wo4. chuck graham (sfmc)	may 1990@	scmc-8906-0001
(x)		

po1. dean king (sfc) (x)	may 1990@	sco-0906-0015
po. chuck stevens (sfc)	may 1990@	sce-0906-0015
sp1 willie stevens (sfc)	may 1990@	sce-8906-0017
ltjg. jason marrs (sfc)	jun 1990@	sco-8906-0018
ltjg. charles finch iii (sfc)	ufp only	
ltjg. james cabaniss (sfc)	ufp only	scs-8908-0004
wo. terry miller (sfc)	ufp only	scs-8908-0004 (x)
wo. deanna winslett (sfc)	ufp only	scm-8907-0005
sfc. richard parker (sfmc) (x)	ufp only	scmc-8907-0004
wo. steve wilkes (sfc)	ufp only	
lt. russell nates (sfc)	ufp only	scss-8908-0006
wo. shelley savage	ufp only	scm-8907-0006
cpl. chuck fair	ufp only	scmc-8908-0005
cpl. jon plant	ufp only	scmc-8908-0007
wo. karren sullivan	oct 1990@	scc-14522-12
wo. kelly spangler	oct 1990	scc-14508-12
ltjg. janet kelley		scc-
cpl. marcus malone	ufp only	scmc-
wo. alen sherwood	ufp only	sco-8908.02
cs. kahuna kite	ufp only	sce-8908-0003
spec. vincent lin	ufp only	sce-8906.23
wo. glen lowe	ufp only	scm-8907-0002
wo3. mike wier	ufp only	scmc-

* denotes vice fleet admiral for ufp
@ denotes dual membership in ufp and starfleet

* denotes vice fleet admiral for ufp
@ denotes dual membership in ufp and starfleet

Note: In the original document, 4 of the above names were indicated as being members of the crew of the 'U.S.S. EXCALIBUR'.

PEA Research (105 Serra Way., Ste. 176., Milpitas, CA. 95035) made the following comments in one of their Files (which consists of collections of large amounts of documents and research related to UFO's):

Ramifications of MJ-12.

If the U.S.A.F. test-flew a disk and was successful, what's to prevent them from using the same saucer to transport men and materials to the moon and mars? They would also be in a position to exploit the archeological artifacts of the pyramids and sphinx in the valley of Illysium on Mars.

If the Canadian Geomagnetic project was successful with their free-energy geomagnetic motor, then why haven't we seen free-energy engines for the home and auto instead of hearing about oil shortages?

If the President of the USA is allowed only certain appointed staff by the Constitution and Congress - are the members of MJ-12 outside of the limits of the Constitution or did Congress give the President the power to set up a Secret Government (non-elected) without the public right to vote on this choice of the governing of the various military and non-military branches of the united states?

When the MJ-12 use non-appropriated funds for their Secret operations are they using money from the Black Budget? If so, when did we cast a vote stating that ANY branch of the Government can use the taxpayers money without giving an account or being held accountable for it?

When MJ-12 refuse to grant FOIA requests because of National Security reasons, is it because the USA won't be secure against foreign earthly powers, alien powers or against the wrath of a misled and deceived United States public (the Voters)?

Can laws be passed to Guarantee that various branches of the Government will be held accountable for (the) shredding of classified documents? How about passing laws to guarantee stiff jail sentences for underlings (secretaries, lower rank personnel) that carry out the command to shred confidential files?

If the top of the mountain is corrupt, what about the foundation that was later raised under it. If a Secret Government is illegal, what about all of the secret projects it started and maintains control of? It's one thing to classify advances in technology as SECRET, but it's quite different to classify non-elected government as SECRET. When that non-accountable Government (non- accountable by reason of being SECRET) passes military laws that affect all branches of Government (military and non-military) are the laws legal or non Constitutional?

If the JMP (Justice for Military Personnel) letter is true, are the actions of the CIA legal as used AGAINST citizens of the USA? Isn't the purpose of the CIA to protect citizens AGAINST foreign threats?

If the MIBS exist according to the documents, what has happened to the Conscience of the Military Personnel that carry out false ID missions against private citizens? Why are Military Personnel carrying out higher up orders to impersonate branches of Government they neither represent or have Rank in? Is this patriotism or blindness?

I used two terms... and the first of these terms is 'government'. We speak of the government as if it is a single thing. It is hardly that. It is actually a hodge-podge of...power-struggling people, but I would like to break it up into two main categories, and that is: 1) The government that we consider to be our duly constituted, our elected and

196

appointed representatives who attempt as best they can to run a semblance of order or Federal government which follows the dictates of the constitution of the United States.

Now that they've failed to do that is not only because they are fallible humans, but also because they are undermined by another government. There is indeed another government operating and that government has immense power and operates primarily behind the scenes. And some other researchers have called it the 'secret government', some have called it the 'high cabal'. And it is a group of people, a very elite group, non-elected, self-appointed people who guide the evolution of (government) policy from behind the scenes. These are people who transcend partisan politics, indeed who transcend the rule of law, and have no thought whatsoever toward the dictates of the constitution.

These are people who regard themselves as the only true guardians or crafters of geo-political reality. And they regard us, indeed they regard elected officials as 'mere mortals'. These people are the self-appointed 'OLYMPIANS'. They have done many things in the name of an agenda which is their own, that we would consider appalling and reprehensible. Indeed things that are criminal, but they're more than criminal because they have sapped and usurped the rights and privileges and the possibilities of our future. These people are running a kind of 'end game' right now. They are trying to determine how 'they' will survive the end time... whether that endtime comes as a kind of biblical apocalypse or...as the catastrophic collapse of the environment... the (so-called) 'population bomb' and all the other things... whether it comes as a collapse of the banking-system which looks to be only days away, or the collapse of the rest of the world's economy -- there are many things that could get us.

"These people in effect are building their own version of 'Noah's Ark'. And that 'Noah's Ark' they're building is underground. Underground bases, indeed all over the world, but particularly here in the United States. Huge underground bases that have actually festooned the underground geography of our continent in a way that would probably stun and shock you. But they even have an underground government, because you see when the government topside is no longer functional because a nuclear bomb lands on Capital Hill, or whether it comes simply because the chaos has reached a point where they must abandon ship, there is preparation as there has been for decades for continuity of government; all the computers, all the personnel are currently in place and operating around the clock. Yes, they are there friends, we have another government in waiting, a government that you never authorized, that you never said we would pay for, that has cost a CALLOSAL FORTUNE, but it's there underground, ready to take over. And indeed, here in our area, I have focused on the Lancaster (CA) area as an example of one of the many... but even in Lancaster in particular, we know for certain are huge underground bases. These are not only places where incredible research is underway but also places where people will go to live when the 'bleep' hits the blades as they say.

"And, these DUMBs and underground enclaves are places that are capable of supporting on an ongoing basis some tens of thousands of people. And so across the country it may be possible to 'save' an 'elect' remnant of some hundreds of thousands of people who will be the 'cream' of the civilization that is meant to survive the apocalypse or the downfall... or whatever it is that's out there getting us. Us 'mere mortals' will have to fend for themselves. The expectation is, part of the end game is, (that those on the surface) will eventually fight each other into a draw or will die of exhaustion or starvation or brutality. And that eventually the 'mere mortals' will (destroy) themselves and rid the world of excess population, so that the 'cream', the 'remnant' will come forward and claim their 'rightful' place... I must say that there is an immense amount of evidence which does support this exact scenario.

FEMA CAMPS' STAGED FOR OFF-MIGRATION, 2009

During the course of the Obama Administraiton FEMA Camps were staging areas for people to "leave Earth" and migrate in ET ships, to other worlds. Tracking this activity was the All Sky Cameras that Astronomical Observatories operate in plain sight. Some of us were monitoring this activity for several years, not recognizing nor understanding, just what we were seeing.

Homeless vagrants and dissidents were rounded up by police, delivered to wilderness FEMA camps, interviewed, and queries whether they would consent to be trafficked elsewhere. I hear about five million Earth humans chose to leave by this meahns. Following are some of the images that All Sky Cameras purveyed on their sites, which showed this activity. I caught images of ships over observatories from 2015 to the present, but I don't know if President Trump is involved.

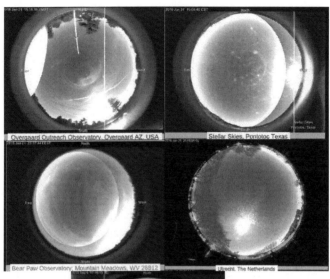

Overgaard Outreach Observatory, Overgaard AZ, USA

Stellar Skies, Pontotoc Texas

Bear Paw Observatory, Mountain Meadows, WV 26812

Utrecht, The Netherlands

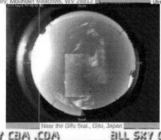

Near the Gifu Stat., Gifu, Japan

all SKY CAM .COM   all SKY CAM .COM

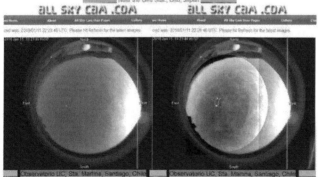

Observatorio UC, Sta. Martina, Santiago, Chile

Observatorio UC, Sta. Martina, Santiago, Chile

200

Population Reduction Policies

Due to pressure of industrial pollution and radiation, Earth itself must be repaired. Two religions are cooperating: Sikhism and Islam. At least two religious ideologies have metastisized into centers of hoarding-by-ego with toxic waste permitted, and they are Zionist Judaism and Calvinist Christianity, that aid and abet and lawfully permit ruination of this world.

Globalists have adopted genocidal methods to rid the world of these wasteful populations from cities and economic centers. However, their tactics of psychological population control have divided the peoples into fighting factions rather than allowed natural and reasonable problem-solving processes to address hoarding, human trafficking, waste and distributive injustices.

So Globalism, in sum, is not helping, and toxic pollution is being increased not abated; ignorance of true situations and matters is increasing, not abated. Divide and conquer is increasing, not abated. Few leaders command sufficient wisdom to "grab their butts with both hands."

Monarchies were disrobed and disempowered a century ago. Special interest groups achieved massive funding to destroy legitimate public process and replace that with formal and interminable Wishing and Wanting.

Natural family planning has been replaced by Hoarding Economics, political polarisation and ignorance of consequences in the quest for pleasure.

One way or another, this plane of suffering humanity will be emptied of further breakage, suffering and want, and those who retire to the wilderness may survive it all, but only those.

5G AND CELLPHONE TOWER EFFECTS.

ROLLOUT OF 5G EFFECTS PREDICTED—

SO THAT PLANETARY EMPTYING CAN PROCEED.

From mainline scientific journals and public sources as well as private sources, we have the complete admitted global master plan of the 5g networks of wireless systems. These are mounted on aircraft passenger aircraft used to distribute a total web of control. Ground-based cell towers, the governmental announces, worldwide ubiquitous, where it's everywhere. Hundreds of mainline studies show that regular cell phone technology for 30 years has been known to cause hundreds of millions of cancers.

5g and it's millimeter waves is even more deadly and actually destroys oxygen carbon dioxide in the atmosphere, and so it will burn the atmosphere including--wait for it--ozone. We have mainline journals of science telling everything. 5G burns the the atmosphere, puts out carbon dioxide that plants need to live. So Officialdumb list that as the toxin and then they create something that destroys oxygen and carbon dioxide. It also destroys water so cells can't absorb water.

Mainstream article after mainstream article, just even from 10 years ago said, cell phones break the DNA, they vibrate the water like a microwave oven. And what's incredible is the government documents that are now out in which it is admitted that it's a depopulation plan, so it sterilizes you, it lowers your fertility, sterilizes, as many causes cancer also do. But also declassified CIA documents in Popular Mechanics just last week admit that they have carrier waves over the millimeter waves that make you sexually aroused, nauseous, depressed, angry--just like the first Kingsman. They just throw it out in Hollywood, and that's how they create scary shows [breaking news, May 3, 2018, from Infowars.--*Editor*]

AFTERWORD

What is missing from this information surpasses what is present. Except for the handful of investigators listed for year 2000+, the suppression of information with respect to ET intrusions is complete.

Nancy Lieder spoke about sky phenomena since 2003 and there is general and mass complaints about chemtrails; but absolutely no accountability for causes, effects and consequences have been published.

We're at a virtual standstill with regard to the secret deals between the West and the ET-Annunaki and Greys by Commercial Treaties in which NO human or natural rights exist.

Human trafficking has become flagrant. Selling children, truants, prisoners, workers, immigrants, body parts and human meat for consumption has become "just bidness." There's a restaurant in LA and one in Tokyo advertising for cannibalism, the new health food.

Police brutality caused by their having non-proportional weapons is a "divide-and-conquer" topic that yields no movement by legislators.

The number of political figures being blackmailed and/or under the influence of bribery, nepotism and perjury escalates daily.

Nibiru has been in our sector of space, as Nancy Lieder says, since 2011, and it has affected our sun, moon and air space. But nobody is talking about any of this.

And as I stated before, ONLY debunking of Flat Earth principles is permitted on Youtube. ONLY propagation of

Globalist Immigration and top-down socialism is permitted by the Vatican. ONLY Big Pharma drugs and vaccines are pushed by HHS. Marijuana the herb is still the reason non-violent felons are serving as slaves in the private prison industry. The number of missing people, missing children, undocumented human beings is exploding, just as the false information filed in Federal records and harassment lawsuits is proliferating.

This listing of missing elements, what is real and what is not real, is why this book is coming out now, so we can all begin to bring ourselves up-to-date.

Rotsa ruck, Friends.

~Emily Windsor-Cragg, May 7, 2018

ADDENDUM, May 9th:

Addition of the plea regarding Planetary Emptying was added as a specific download and as a specific 'demand' for service. I don't know what else I can say about it. Interplanetary migration has been where and for what purpose the 'disappeared' have been salvaged and conserved, whose lifestyle do not and will not conflict with the 'Prime Directive,' as a soul, as a hominid, or as an Earth human. By the way, if you do not already know the Earth is a dome-covered plane situated on a sheet of ice, you are too ignorant to belong to a civil society.

~Emily Windsor-Cragg, May 9, 2018

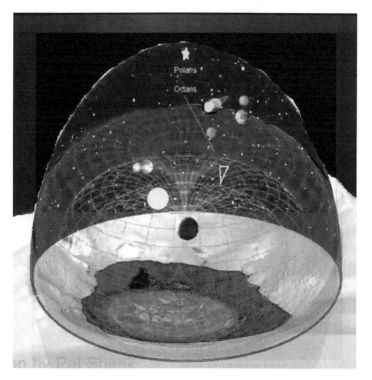

Anybody who can believe that oceans stick to the bottom of a sphere simply doesn't have his eyes or mind working competently.

Rotsa ruck, Deceived Ones.

Made in the USA
Middletown, DE
04 June 2022